Praise for *Compelling Conversations: Questions and Quotations for Advanced Vietnamese English Language Learners*

"Compelling Conversations is a great book to get my students to talk beyond the usual topics they find in ESL textbooks in Vietnam. The topics encourage students to think, discuss, and exchange ideas and their own personal interpretations of idioms, quotes and proverbs. This is a welcome break from the somewhat rigid or structured speaking and listening books that we have used before. My students from Korea and Turkey also use this book as the main text in our Free Talking class. If you want to have your students talking and conversing, this book is a must-have! This book is also a big help in exposing our ELL students in Vietnam to quotes that are often used in SAT type essay prompts."

Leah Montano, ELD Program Coordinator
APU International School
Ho Chi Minh City, Vietnam

Reviews for Compelling Conversations: Questions & Quotations on Timeless Topics

… highly effective

"In my own teaching, I have found questions and quotations to be highly effective in promoting student discussion. Questions are useful in that they require a response from the listener. Asking them also helps students master the tricky rules of the interrogative. Quotations are brilliant flashes of wit expressed in the shortest space possible, often just a sentence or two. The authors have compiled a formidable collection of quotations by famous people."

"The authors also add some wise proverbs here and there. My two favourites were "Recite `patience' three times and it will spare you a murder" and "When money talks, truth keeps silent", which are from Korea and Russia.

In sum, Compelling Conversations is a recommended resource for teachers who want to make their conversation classes more learner-centered. It should be especially appealing to those who wish to escape the confines of the Presentation-Practice-Production approach and do without a formal grammatical or functional syllabus. It reflects the authors' considerable professional experience, and would be a notable addition to any English teacher's bookshelf."

Hall Houston
English Teaching Professional magazine (January 2009)

…wonderful

"A wonderful source of materials triggering authentic (not stilted) communication."

Dr. Sharon Myers, Lecturer
American Language Institute
University of Southern California

… natural conversations

"The students I tutor are well-educated adults, rich in culture and experiences. This book allows them to produce natural conversations using what is most intimate to them: their lives and their culture."

Patricia Schulze, ESL Tutor

...engaging and interesting

"These conversation starters are not just for ESL students but for anyone who is a bit shy or has trouble speaking around people. The questions are engaging and interesting and draws people into a variety of diverse subjects. The book also has many jokes, quotes and proverbs that often bring common day English into the mix. A must have book!"

Susan Specter
Artist and EFL tutor

...allows students to learn by speaking

"Immigrants need to feel comfortable speaking English, but too often students learn everything except conversation in ESL classrooms. Compelling Conversations allows students to learn by speaking."

Zigmund Vays, Founder/President
Community Enhancement Services College
Los Angeles

"This outstanding resource (Compelling Conversations) allows teachers to confidently walk into an advanced ESL classroom with self-contained, engaging conversation lessons. The 45 thematic chapters allow you to both evoke student experience with long lists of practical and savvy questions.

The inclusion of global proverbs and classic quotations also provides larger cultural contexts to inspire deeper conversations - or writing assignments. Students should also appreciate the generous amount of authentic language. I wish I would have had that book in my old adult/university classes. A great book for adult education teachers, university instructors, and private tutors!"

Eric Busch, Director/Founder
ESLHQ.com (August 2007)

...excellent!

"This book is excellent! Both teachers and students love it."

Marina Goldshteyn, Director
Community Enhancement Services College

...a welcome addition

"Have you been looking for a good ESL manual? This manual (*Compelling Conversations: Questions and Quotations on Timeless Topics*) helps conversation by giving common subjects to talk about."

"Since English is one of the more confusing, difficult and strange languages for a foreigner to grasp and be comfortable conversing in, the compilers pack in 45 chapters over 30 questions, 10 or more targeted vocabulary words, some proverbs, and quotations per chapter. Each chapter focuses on a promising conversation topic. They start with easy questions and continue on to questions a bit more abstract. Each question is there to allow the speaker to share his life experiences along with his insights."

This manual will go best with the advanced ESL student or even at coffee shop conversation clubs. It will bring about authentic, not stilted communication, which should be the purpose of an ESL course. It is easier for a person to learn a language through conversation rather than by a given list of vocabulary words. That is what makes this a welcome addition which can be used by people who must learn English to advance in the world."

Dane Robert Swanson
Santa Monica Daily Press (1/16/2009)

...hours of conversation practice

"I wish I had written this book! It will provide students with hours of conversation practice."

Nina Ito
California State University Teacher and Co-author of
The Great Big BINGO Book: Bingo Games for ESL Learners

COMPELLING CONVERSATIONS

Questions & Quotations for Advanced Vietnamese
English Language Learners – Volume 1

Written, Compiled, and Edited by
Eric H. Roth and Toni Aberson

Roth, Eric Hermann, 1961-
Compelling conversations. Volume 1 / written,
compiled and edited by Eric H. Roth and Toni Aberson.
p. cm.
Includes bibliographical references.
Subtitle: Questions and quotations for advanced
Vietnamese English language learners.
LCCN 2011920242
ISBN-13: 9780982617816
ISBN-10: 098261781X

1. English language--Textbooks for foreign speakers--
Vietnamese. 2. English language--Conversation and
phrase books--Vietnamese. 3. Quotations, English.
I. Aberson, Toni. II. Title. III. Title: Questions and\
quotations for advanced Vietnamese English language
learners.

PE1130.V5R68 2011   428.3'495922
QBI11-600002

Editorial Advisor Steven J. Riggs
Photographs by Laurie Selik and iStockphoto.com. Cover Image from iStockphoto.com

To order additional copies, share comments, ask questions or contribute quotations, please visit www.
compellingconversations.com. Or email eric@compellingconversations.com.

Chimayo Press
3766 Redwood Avenue
Los Angeles, California 90066-3506
United States of America

+1.310.390.0131
www.CompellingConversations.com

Dedicated to
Dani Herbert Joseph Roth
(1937—1997)

A global citizen, he could talk with almost anyone, in six different languages, and share a laugh. This book attempts to capture some of his generous spirit, wit, and curiosity.

...and to the resilient people of Vietnam

"Kindness is the language which the deaf can hear and the blind can see."
—Mark Twain (1835-1910), American author

"One cannot always be a hero, but one can always be human."
—Johann Wolfgang von Goethe ((1749-1832),
German playwright, novelist, and scientist

Acknowledgements

> **"Gratitude is the memory of the heart."**
>
> —French proverb

> **"No one is as capable of gratitude as one who has emerged from the kingdom of the night."**
>
> —Elie Wiesel (1928–), American writer and Nobel Peace Prize winner

Several educators, friends, and colleagues have helped in the creation of this new conversation textbook for Vietnamese students. Numerous English language professionals and students have made sensible suggestions at critical moments. Allow me to publicly thank a few of you by name.

Toni Aberson

Laurie Selik

Dr. Binh Tran

Mai-Anh Nwin

Steven J. Riggs

Kaycee Huynh

Tram Tan

Hung Ngoc. Nguyen

Michael Dang

Leah Montano

Tran Nguyen Yen Le

Mai-Khanh Nguyen

Emily Borden

Paula Johnson

I remain especially grateful to five individuals: Dr. Binh Tran, Mai-Anh Nwin, Steve Riggs, Emily Borden and Paula Johnson. Dr. Binh provided the opportunity to transform an ESL book for American immigrants into a specialized EFL textbook. Mai-Anh recognized the tremendous potential for an engaging communicative textbook and shared her vision of what is possible. Steve edited the entire book, asked many questions and always believed in the book's potential. Emily oversaw the early draft in Ho Chi Minh City and helped further revise it in Los Angeles. Finally, Paula brought all the editorial and design elements together.

Several other Vietnamese educators, EFL professionals, fellow English teachers, and Vietnamese-American friends made helpful suggestions and shared their insights. This book came into existence thanks to the friendly spirit of collaboration and conversation. It's a pleasure to acknowledge their efforts. I must especially thank my co-author and mother Toni Aberson for her creative contributions to *Compelling Conversations*. Let me also thank Laurie Selik, my publishing partner and wonderful wife, for her dedication, focus and sophistication.

Finally, I would like to thank the dedicated English students who worked with me during the last decade. From Ho Chi Minh City to Santa Monica College to the University of Southern California, you have shared your insights and created compelling classroom conversations. Naturally, I take full responsibility for any mistakes, omissions, or imperfections.

May we all keep learning and sharing as our world continues to rapidly change in the 21st century.

Eric H. Roth

Introduction

To the Students:

Why do you want to learn English? Are you planning on entering an excellent university or meeting new international friends? Are you looking to make more money with international business or travel? Do you want a better job, a high TOEFL score, or a nursing career? Speaking clear English and creating smart conversations can open many doors for you in Vietnam and around the world.

This conversation textbook will gently push you to develop many vital skills:

- Speak English
- Listen to English
- Respond to both questions and comments
- Ask questions
- Learn and use new vocabulary words
- Paraphrase proverbs
- Discuss quotations
- Make judgments
- Support statements and opinions
- Develop critical thinking skills
- Begin conversations with native English speakers

We learn by talking and listening to each other. We learn by doing and practicing. Sometimes we have short talks; sometime we have long conversations. Sometimes we speak Vietnamese; sometimes we speak English.

Together, we will talk about many things in English and discuss many topics in this class in English. We will ask questions in English. We will answer questions in English, too. We will use simple and more difficult words in English. We learn traditional sayings and modern expressions. We will learn—and use—new English vocabulary words in our conversation class. Step by step, we will know more English words and how to ask more questions so we can build better conversations in English.

Learning to speak English requires us to speak English in every class. So, we will talk about our present lives and reflect on our past experiences in interview and small group discussions. We will also share our hopes and plans for the future. By telling our personal stories and sharing our ideas, we will also create compelling conversations together—in English.

Shall we begin?

Eric Roth and Toni Aberson
Co-authors, *Compelling Conversations*

www.CompellingConversations.com

Contents

CHAPTER 1
GETTING STARTED

Speaking English allows you to be yourself in an international language. Throughout these lessons, you will work with other students. You will be asking questions about their experiences, and you will be answering questions which they ask you. In this way, you will be practicing English, learning about other cultures, and practicing ways to make conversation pleasant and interesting. You will create compelling conversations in English.

MEETING EACH OTHER
Divide into small groups. Big journeys begin with small steps. Go around the group and please answer these three questions.

• What's your name?

• Where do you speak English now?

• Why do you want to speak better English?

In this class, we want to encourage each other. Smiling and keeping eye contact in many English countries is a way to encourage. Frowning or looking away when others are speaking can discourage people. Carefully listen to each other.

ENCOURAGING EACH OTHER
Words can also show that we want others to feel comfortable speaking. In your group, take turns saying each of the following statements. Give eye contact to others as you speak. This practice will make it easier to use these encouraging statements in your conversations with others.

• That is interesting.	• Cool.
• You are right!	• What happened next?
• Can you explain more?	• Please continue.
• I like that!	• I enjoy listening to what you have to say.

Take turns telling your classmates two things that you like and why.

I like _____ because _____.

I like _____ because _____.

Other group members can say encouraging phrases to keep the conversation going.

English is a crazy, difficult, and often confusing language. English is sometimes frustrating because many words sound different than they "should" from the spelling. You will be asked to write questions in each chapter, but you can use your dictionary to check spellings. Electronic dictionaries can also allow you to hear words. You can keep a spelling and vocabulary log to help you remember the correct spelling, too.

"Nothing in life is be feared. It is only to be understood."

—Marie Curie (1867-1934), physicist

PRONUNCIATION TIPS

Some students, however, make English more difficult by expecting themselves to be perfect and speak exactly like a native English speaker. That's a noble goal, but a very, very difficult goal.

For now, a more important goal is to speak in a clear, natural way so your listeners can understand your words and ideas. Remember that English speakers also have many different accents—especially in the United States. Therefore, we will focus much more on natural, clear speech than perfect pronunciation. Being understood matters most.

However, using a few techniques will often improve your English pronunciation:

• Open the mouth wider to speak English than Vietnamese.

• Speak slower.

• Pay attention to word endings.

Feel free to ask your partner to repeat a word or sentence if you do not understand. Americans do this all the time if they do not understand a question. "Can you repeat that?" and "Please speak slower" are very helpful phrases.

PARAPHRASING PROVERBS

Proverbs, or traditional sayings, can show big ideas in a few words. We will use proverbs and famous quotations so we can look at the ideas of many people and cultures, and discuss these ideas. We will also often paraphrase proverbs and discuss quotations to expand our vocabulary.

Paraphrasing is the ability to say what something means using different words.

Paraphrasing is an important skill in both writing and speaking. In this exercise, please take turns reading the quotations and proverbs out loud. What do they mean? As a group, paraphrase each proverb by using different words to show the same idea. Remember to encourage each other with words and gestures.

• Words are free so choose kind words when you speak.—Vietnamese

• You catch more flies with honey than with vinegar.

• I hear and I forget. I see and I remember. I do and I understand. —Chinese

• We learn by doing.—English

• Speech is silver, but silence is golden.—Vietnamese

• You know enough if you know how to learn.—Greek

• There is only one beautiful child in the world, and each mother has that one. —Latin American

• Keep it light, bright and polite.—English

⭐ **THINK ABOUT IT...**

What words do you find hard to say in English?

....

....

....

www.CompellingConversations.com

DISCUSSING QUOTATIONS

In your group, read aloud each of the following quotations. Decide among yourselves what you think the quotation means. Then, talk about how the meaning of the quotation will help you work well with the other students in this class. Remember to practice using encouraging gestures and words with each other.

- "Courtesy costs nothing."
  —Ralph Waldo Emerson (1803–1882), American writer, philosopher

- "I never know how much of what I say is true."
  —Bette Midler (1945-), American singer and actress

- "The secret of education is respecting the pupil."
  —Ralph Waldo Emerson (1803–1882), American poet, philosopher

- "It is not best that we should all think alike; it is a difference of opinion which makes horse races."
  —Mark Twain (1835–1910), American writer, humorist

- "I am tomorrow, or some future day, what I establish today. I am today what I established yesterday or some previous day."
  —James Joyce (1882–1941), Irish novelist

EXPANDING OUR VOCABULARY

agree   argue   conversation   courage   disagree

discourage   encourage   gesture   proverb   quotation

Agree, *verb*: to think the same way as someone else.

• I agree with you.

argue, *verb*: to give reasons and strongly disagree.

• Chau argued with Trang over the quickest way home in the rain.

conversation, *noun*: talking; exchanging words between two or more people.

• We have long conversations because we can talk about so many topics together.

courage, *noun*: bravery, the act of facing danger.

• The little mouse showed a lot of courage when he approached the lion.

disagree, *verb*: to think in a different way; to not agree.

• We disagree about the best place to go fishing at night in Vietnam.

discourage, *verb*: to make someone feel bad about doing something; to advise against.

• My father discouraged me from smoking by explaining how harmful and dangerous it is long-term for my heart, lungs and general health.

encourage, *verb*: to make someone feel good about an action; to say "yes, you can."

• The basketball coach encourages all his players to always do their best.

⭐ ON YOUR OWN

People communicate with words 24 hours a day, seven days a week. During the next 24 hours, please carefully observe people talking to each other.

Note their communication style, gestures, and word choices. You can watch people in stores, on buses, at school and even on TV.

Prepare three observations to share with the class:

1. ....
....
....

2. ....
....
....

3. ....
....
....

gesture, *noun*: a motion or movement of a part of the body.

• The child bowed his head in a gesture of respect and obedience.

proverb, *noun*: a popular, wise, or traditional saying; a well-known phrase.

• The proverb "actions speak louder than words" means what you do is more important than what you say.

quotation, *noun*: a person's exact words; a passage from a book or speech; a famous saying.

• "We have nothing to fear but fear itself," is a famous quotation by Franklin D. Roosevelt, a popular American President. *Grammar note: Quotation marks (" ") at beginning and end of a sentence or paragraph indicate that it is a direct quotation.*

ASKING QUESTIONS

Asking questions is an essential skill in creating quality conversations. This activity also provides a chance to review your English vocabulary. The grammar used with questions can also be difficult in English. You will be asked in every chapter to write five questions using the vocabulary words. Your teacher can check your sentences for proper grammar.

A. Select five vocabulary words in this chapter, and write a question for each word. Remember to start your question with a question word (Who, What, Where, When, Why, How, Is, Are, Do, Did, Does, etc). You also want to end each question with a question mark (?). Underline each vocabulary word.

Example: How do parents encourage their children?

1...
2...
3...
4...
5...

B. Take turns asking and answering questions with your partner or group members. Ask your teacher to give you feedback on your questions to check your English grammar.

SHARING ENGLISH CONVERSATION CLASS TIPS

With the other members in your group, make a list of five or more important rules to follow which will help you create pleasant conversations.

Examples: Speak clearly. Do the homework.

1. ....
2. ....
3. ....
4. ....
5. ....

⭐ TIPS

Here are some tips for building good conversations:

• Be active
• Be curious
• Be encouraging
• Be kind
• Be open
• Be tolerant
• Be yourself

4

DISCUSSING QUOTATIONS

Quotations appear frequently throughout this book. Reading the ideas of other people and other cultures helps you look at many ways of thinking and introduces you to some famous people.

Take turns reading these quotations out loud, and discuss them with your partner. Do you agree with the quotation? Disagree? Why? Mark your answer.

1. "Conversation means being able to disagree and still continue the conversation."
   —Dwight MacDonald (1906–1982), American editor

   ☐ Agree ☐ Disagree Why? ....

2. "Speech is civilization itself…It is silence which isolates."
   —Thomas Mann (1875–1955), German writer

   ☐ Agree ☐ Disagree Why? ....

3. "If it is language that makes us human, one half of language is to listen."
   —Jacob Trapp (1899–1992), American orator

   ☐ Agree ☐ Disagree Why? ....

4. "Argument is the worst form of conversation."
   —Jonathon Swift (1667–1745), English writer, satirist

   ☐ Agree ☐ Disagree Why? ....

5. "Life shrinks or expands in proportion to one's courage."
   —Anaïs Nin (1903–1977), French-American author

   ☐ Agree ☐ Disagree Why? ....

6. "Man does not speak because he thinks; he thinks because he speaks. Or rather, speaking is no different than thinking: to speak is to think."
   —Octavio Paz, (1914–1998), Mexican writer, Nobel Prize winner (1990)

   ☐ Agree ☐ Disagree Why? ....

7. "Show me someone who never gossips and I'll show you someone who isn't interested in people."
   —Barbara Walters (1929-), American TV journalist

   ☐ Agree ☐ Disagree Why? ....

8. "It is easier to confess a defect than to claim a quality."
   —Max Beerbohm (1876-1956), English humorist and essayist

   ☐ Agree ☐ Disagree Why? ....

⭐ ON YOUR OWN

Please write a quotation that you like and tell us why.

A Favorite Quotation:

....

....

....

....

....

Why? ....

....

....

....

....

Chapter Notes

CHAPTER 2
GOING BEYOND HELLO

TELLING YOUR STORY

Please interview the person sitting next to you. Feel free to add or omit any questions that you want. Take turns talking, write notes, and prepare to introduce your partner to our class. Let's begin!

1. What's your full name? How do you spell that?

2. Who chose your name? Why?

3. Where were you born? Were you the first child? Second? Fifth?

4. Do you have any older brothers? Sisters? Younger siblings?

5. Where did you grow up? Is that a city, village, or suburb?

6. How would you describe yourself as a child? Why?

7. Do you have a favorite possession? Why?

8. Where do you live?

9. Do you have a favorite color? Number? Season? Why?

10. What kind of music do you listen to? Do you have a favorite singer? Group?

11. What's your favorite radio station or television channel? Why?

12. What movies can you recommend? Why do you like those films?

EXPANDING OUR VOCABULARY

Please circle the words that you know. Ask your partner or teacher for the meanings of the other words.

appreciate	enthusiasm	frown	goal	hobby
impression	interview	possession	recommend	sibling

appreciate, *verb*: to feel thankful for something, to like and see the value in something.

• She appreciates your friendship.

enthusiasm, *noun*: excitement; a passion for someone or something.

• He showed his enthusiasm by loudly cheering for the local sports team.

frown, *noun*: a face of sadness or disapproval where the mouth widens downward at both ends; *verb*: to show unhappiness or displeasure with the face; the opposite of smile.

• Her frown showed her displeasure with her poor test results.

• She frowned in the mirror, but smiled when she saw her best friend.

goal, *noun*: a target, a desired result.

• The goal is to get at least 100 on the TOEFL exam.

hobby, *noun*: an activity done for fun, not for money; a desired way to spend time and relax.

• His favorite hobbies are playing computer games and taking photographs.

impression, *noun*: a mental "picture" left by a person, place, or thing in another's mind.

• Make a good impression on your supervisor if you want a better job.

interview, *noun*: a formal conversation.

verb: to ask someone questions to gain more information.

• My job interview lasted 20 minutes, and the manager wants to interview me again next week.

possession *noun*: holding or owning an object.

• Her favorite possession is a ring that her grandmother gave her years ago.

recommend, verb: to advise, to give your opinion

• I recommend you try the delicious shrimp soup.

sibling, *noun*: brother or sister in the same family.

• I have two siblings: a younger brother and an older sister.

smile, *noun*: an expression of happiness where the mouth widens upward at both ends; *verb*: to display happiness or pleasure with the face — the opposite of frown.

• He has a wonderful smile!

• Thuy smiles so broadly you can see all her teeth.

suburb, *noun*: an area where people live outside a city

• I work in the city, but I live in a small suburb where it's quiet and cheaper.

ASKING QUESTIONS

A. Select five vocabulary words in this chapter, and write a question for each word. Remember to start your question with a question word (Who, What, Where, When, Why, How, Is, Are, Do, Did, Does, etc). You also want to end each question with a question mark (?). Underline each vocabulary word.

Example: Can you recommend a good restaurant?

1. ....

2. ....

3. ....

4. ....

5. ....

B. Take turns asking and answering questions with your partner or group members.

"Accept me as I am—only then will we discover each other."

—Federico Fellini (1920-1993), Italian director/screenwriter

PARAPHRASING PROVERBS
Read the proverbs below.

- Those who are good in mind are better than those who are good in appearance. —Vietnamese

- Strangers are just friends you haven't met yet.—American

- Beauty is a good letter of recommendation.—German

- You never get a second chance to make a first impression.—American

- You're never too old to learn.—Latin

- A single conversation across the table with a wise person is worth a month's study of books.—Chinese

- Chewing, one eats. Reflecting, one speaks.—Vietnamese

THE CONVERSATION CONTINUES...
1. What do you like to do outside? Why?

2. Where do you walk, hike, jog, or bike on the weekends?

3. What's your favorite sport? Why?

4. How do you like to spend your free time? What interests you?

5. Do you have a hobby? How long have you enjoyed it?

6. How long have you studied English? Where?

7. Where do you usually speak English? Why?

8. What makes you smile? Where do you feel most comfortable?

9. What are some things that might cause you to frown?

10. How do you express enthusiasm in a word or sound in Vietnamese?

11. Do you have a favorite English or Vietnamese word or expression? Why?

12. What are your goals for this year? Why? What's your plan?

13. How would your friends describe you? What would you add?

14. What are three things that you appreciate about living in Vietnam?

DISCUSSING QUOTATIONS
Take turns reading these quotations out loud, and discuss them with your partner. Do you agree with the quotation? Disagree? Why? Mark your answer.

1. "I never met a man I didn't like."
   —Will Rogers (1879–1935), American humorist

   ☐ Agree ☐ Disagree Why? ....

2. "I am free of all prejudices. I hate every one equally."
   —W. C. Fields (1880–1946), American actor/comedian

   ☐ Agree ☐ Disagree Why? ....

REMEMBER...
- Be encouraging
- Be kind
- Be open

3. "There is no such thing as a worthless conversation, provided you know what to listen for. And questions are the breath of life for a conversation."
—James Nathan Miller (1953-), American contemporary journalist

☐ Agree ☐ Disagree Why? ....

4. "Conversation is an art in which a man has all mankind for his competitors, for it is that which all are practicing every day while they live."
—Ralph Waldo Emerson (1803–1882), American essayist/philosopher

☐ Agree ☐ Disagree Why? ....

5. "The true spirit of conversation consists in building on another man's observation, not overturning it."
—Edward G. Bulwer-Lytton (1803–1873), British novelist/politician

☐ Agree ☐ Disagree Why? ....

6. "Confidence contributes more to conversation than wit."
—Francois de La Rochefoucauld (1613–1680), French writer

☐ Agree ☐ Disagree Why? ....

7. "It takes two to speak truth—one to speak and another to hear."
—Henry David Thoreau (1817–1862), American philosopher

☐ Agree ☐ Disagree Why? ....

8. "I am simple, complex, generous, selfish, unattractive, beautiful, lazy and driven."
—Barbara Streisand (1942–), American singer, actress, director, producer

☐ Agree ☐ Disagree Why? ....

9. "Everything becomes a little different as soon as it is spoken out loud."
—Hermann Hesse (1877–1962), novelist

☐ Agree ☐ Disagree Why? ....

10. "Never let your fear of striking out get in your way."
—Babe Ruth (1895–1948), American baseball legend

☐ Agree ☐ Disagree Why? ....

11. "It was impossible to get a conversation going; everybody was talking too much."
—Yogi Berra (1925–) legendary baseball manager/catcher

☐ Agree ☐ Disagree Why? ....

⭐ GOALS

Places I want to speak English:

1. ....

2. ....

3. ....

www.CompellingConversations.com

chapter Notes

CHAPTER 3

BEING HOME

SHARING EXPERIENCES

Everybody lives somewhere. Share the story of your home with a conversation partner by responding to these questions. Feel free to add other questions.

1. Do you live in a house or an apartment?

2. How long have you lived there?

3. Why did you choose your current home? What attracted you?

4. Did you have a checklist when looking for a home? What was on it?

5. What legal documents did you have to sign before moving in? Lease? Mortgage? Other? Did you have to pay any fees?

6. What do you like about it? How long did it take you to make a decision?

7. What do you dislike about it? What, if anything, annoys you?

8. Which is your favorite room? Why? What does it look like?

9. Which room is the heart of your current home? Kitchen? TV room?

10. What changes have you made to this residence? Paint? Repairs?

11. What further changes would you like to make?

12. What paintings, posters, or other artwork do you have?

13. Do you have any pets? What's their favorite spot?

14. What, if any, plants or flowers do you have? Where are they?

15. By the way, how did you find your current home? Word of mouth? Ad?

EXPANDING VOCABULARY

Which words do you already know? Working with your partner, use each of the vocabulary words in a sentence.

appliance	checklist	exterior	fee	homesick
interior	lease	neighbor	neighborhood	residence

appliance *noun*: a machine or device that performs particular functions in the office or home; an object with a special use or purpose.

• Her family had a coffee-maker and a toaster, but still needed a TV and other appliances at home.

checklist *noun*: a written series of items arranged top to bottom, created to insure accuracy or completeness.

• Nga always kept a checklist of what she needed from the store because it was far from her house.

> "The strength of the nation derives from the integrity of the home."
>
> —Confucius (551-479 B.C.E), Chinese philosopher

exterior *adjective*: the outside; opposite of interior

• Exterior paint must be stronger than interior paint because it must protect against the rain.

fee *noun*: money paid for a service; the cost to use something of value owned by someone else.

• You have to pay a fee to register a motorcycle in Ho Chi Minh City.

homesick *adjective*: feeling lonely, missing one's family or home.

• She got homesick for her family after two weeks away.

interior *noun*: the inside of a house, room, object or area; the inner part of a place or thing.

• The bright interior colors gave the new restaurant a modern, hip look.

lease *noun*: a contract made to obtain the use of something (home, business, car) for a specified price over a specified period of time; a period of time covered by a lease; verb to rent or lease

• My apartment lease ends next month.

neighbor *noun*: a person living next door or nearby

• The neighbor feeds the cats when I leave town.

neighborhood *noun*: a particular section of a city;

• They liked the neighborhood because it had a lovely park and a good school.

residence *noun*: a place one lives; the act or fact of living in a specific place as one's home.

• My school residence is in Hanoi where I study, but I feel like my true home is back home with my family.

ASKING QUESTIONS

A. Select five vocabulary words in this chapter, and write a question for each word. Remember to start your question with a question word (Who, What, Where, When, Why, How, Is, Are, Do, Did, Does, etc.). You also want to end each question with a question mark (?). Underline each vocabulary word.

Example: Is this a new appliance?

1..

2..

3..

4..

5..

B. Take turns asking and answering questions with your partner or group members. Ask your teacher to give you feedback on your questions to check your English grammar.

A good neighbor is a found treasure.

—Vietnamese

⭐ ON YOUR OWN

Can you add two more proverbs about homes?

- ....
....

- ....
....

PARAPHRASING PROVERBS

What do these proverbs and sayings mean? Discuss them with your partner. Circle your favorite.

- East or West, home is best.—Vietnamese
- Home is where the heart is.
- Home is where we grumble the most and are treated the best.
- Birds return to old nests.—Japanese
- A house is not a home.
- Settling in a good home brings forth prosperity.—Vietnamese
- Anger in a home is like rottenness in a fruit.
- A good neighbor is a found treasure.—Vietnamese

THE CONVERSATION CONTINUES...

1. When you were a child, did you live in a house or an apartment?
2. How long did you live in one residence?
3. What did you like about it? What did you dislike?
4. With whom did you live as a child?
5. Which was your favorite room? Why?
6. Which room was the heart of your childhood home?
7. Have you ever felt homesick? What did you miss the most?
8. What is your favorite childhood memory at home?
9. Is your old neighborhood the same today as it was when you were a child?
10. Would you like to live there now? Why or why not?
11. Would you rather live in an apartment or a house? Why?
12. Would you rather live in a city, a suburb, a small town, or the countryside? Why?
13. Can you suggest some places to find interior design ideas?
14. What would your dream residence be like? Can you describe it in detail?
15. What modern appliances would your dream house have?
16. Do you see homes as a good investment? Why?
17. Would you rather put money in a home or in a bank? Why?
18. What makes a house a home for you?

DISCUSSING QUOTATIONS

Take turns reading these quotations out loud, and discuss them with your partner. Do you agree with the quotation? Disagree? Why? Mark your answer.

1. "He is happiest, be he king or peasant, who finds peace in his home."
   —Johann Wolfgang von Goethe (1749–1832), German playwright

   ☐ Agree ☐ Disagree Why? ....

2. "A man's home is his castle."
   —Sir Edward Coke (1552–1634), English lord/statesman

   ☐ Agree ☐ Disagree Why? ....

3. "Home: The place where when you have to go there, they have to take you in."
   —Robert Frost (1875–1963), American poet

   ☐ Agree ☐ Disagree Why? ....

4. "A house is not a home unless it contains food and fire for the mind as well as the body."
   —Benjamin Franklin (1706-1790), American statesman

   ☐ Agree ☐ Disagree Why? ....

5. "Determine what sort of a house will be fit for you; determine to work for it, and to get one that you can entirely enjoy and manage."
   —John Ruskin (1819-1900), English critic

   ☐ Agree ☐ Disagree Why? ....

6. "No matter under what circumstances you leave it, home does not cease to be home. No matter how you lived there—well or poorly."
   —Joseph Brodsky (1940–1996), Russian-American writer/poet, Nobel Prize winner (1987)

   ☐ Agree ☐ Disagree Why? ....

7. "Home is the girl's prison and the woman's workhouse."
   —George Bernard Shaw (1856–1950), Irish writer/playwright, Nobel Prize winner (1925)

   ☐ Agree ☐ Disagree Why? ....

8. "The best way to keep children at home is make the home atmosphere pleasant, and let the air out of the tires."
   —Dorothy Parker (1893–1967), American writer

   ☐ Agree ☐ Disagree Why? ....

9. "Modern apartments are built on the principle that half as much room should cost twice as much money."
   —Evan Esar (1899–1995), American humorist

   ☐ Agree ☐ Disagree Why? ....

10. "Have nothing in your house that you do not know to be useful, or believe to be beautiful."
    —William Morris (1834-1896), English artist and writer

    ☐ Agree ☐ Disagree Why? ....

✪ ON YOUR OWN

Select five adjectives (spacious, cozy) for your dream home:

1. ....

2. ....

3. ....

4. ....

5. ....

Let's expand your dream. Use the worksheet "My Dream Home" (on the next page.) Share your dream with your classmates in the next class.

My Dream Home

Student Name .... Class ....

Teacher: .... Date ....

What is your dream home? Please use your knowledge and research to describe your dream home that you would like to live in. Use the vocabulary learned in this lesson. Use your imagination. Dream big!

Location ....

1. What does the outside look like? ....

....

....

2. How many rooms are there? ....

3. Describe the kitchen: ....

....

....

4. Describe your room: ....

....

....

5. Describe the living room: ....

....

....

6. Describe another room: ....

....

7. What else makes this home special? ....

....

....

8. What other information or details can you share? ....

....

....

Be prepared to share your dream with your classmates!

Chapter Notes

....

....

....

....

....

....

....

....

....

....

....

....

....

....

....

....

....

....

....

....

....

....

....

....

....

....

....

....

....

CHAPTER 4
DESCRIBING FAMILY TIES

SHARING EXPERIENCES

Family remains the center of society. Share your experiences and discover your partner's many experiences as a family member.

1. Do you have a large, medium, or small family?
   How many people are in your family?

2. What are your parents' names? How do you spell their names?

3. Where were your parents born? Were they born in a hospital?

4. How did your parents meet? What attracted them to each other?

5. How long did they know each other before they got married?

6. Do you know how old your parents were when they got married?

7. How many siblings do you have? Are you the oldest? Youngest?

8. What do you enjoy doing with your siblings?

9. Do you live with your nuclear family or your extended family?
   With whom do you live now?

10. Does your extended family have a leader or dominant figure?
    Is there a patriarch or a matriarch?

11. How many aunts and uncles do you have?

12. Which aunt or uncle is your favorite? Why?

13. What language or languages did you hear in your childhood home?
    Which languages are spoken now?

14. Do you exchange gifts on holidays? Which holidays?

15. Who gives the best gifts in your family? Why?

16. What do you appreciate about your family?

17. How can families provide comfort?

EXPANDING VOCABULARY

ancestor	extended	half-brother	in-law	matriarch
nuclear	patriarch	reunion	spouse	step-sister

ancestor *noun*: an early member of the family, clan, or tribe.

• My ancestors came from Hanoi.

extended family *noun*: a large family with aunts, uncles, cousins, grandparents.

• Our extended families attended the huge wedding party in Dalat.

A drop of blood is worth more than a lake of water.

—Vietnamese

www.CompellingConversations.com

half-brother *noun*: a male sibling who has just one parent in common with other siblings.

- Steve was my half-brother; we shared the same mother, but had different fathers.

in-law *noun*: member of the family through marriage; a relative due to marriage.

- I love my mother-in-law, and respect my father-in-law.

matriarch *noun*: the female head of a family.

- My grandmother is the matriarch of our family and hosts our family gatherings.

nuclear family *noun*: a single family group: a family unit of only parents and children.

- A typical nuclear family might be a father, mother, and two children.

patriarch *noun*: the male head of a family; a man who is the ruler of his extended family.

- The family patriarch makes many family decisions and is respected.

reunion *noun*: a gathering of people who have been separated.

- Our extended family meets for holidays and weddings, but we also have an official reunion every five years.

spouse *noun*: a wife or husband.

- My spouse is my husband, my best friend, and the father of my children.

stepsister *noun*: the daughter of one's stepmother or stepfather.

- My stepsister and I became good friends.

ASKING QUESTIONS

A. Select five vocabulary words in this chapter, and write a question for each word. Remember to start your question with a question word (Who, What, Where, When, Why, How, Is, Are, Do, Did, Does, etc). You also want to end each question with a question mark (?). Underline each vocabulary word.

Example: Do many extended families live in the village?

1. ....

2. ....

3. ....

4. ....

5. ....

B. Take turns asking and answering questions with your partner or group members. Ask your teacher for feedback on your English grammar.

★ REMEMBER...

- Listen carefully.
- Speak clearly.
- Skip awkward questions.

PARAPHRASING PROVERBS

Take turns reading the proverbs below out loud. Circle your favorite and explain why. Can you add one more?

- Half of your fortune lies in your family line.—Korean

- Of all the virtues, family duty is the first.—Chinese

- A brother helped by a brother is like a fortified city.—Latin

- Like father, like son.—Latin

- A good husband makes a good wife.—Vietnamese

- Whoever marries for money will have unworthy children.—Russian

- A drop of blood is worth more than a lake of water.—Vietnamese

- Brothers and sisters are as close as hands and feet.—Vietnamese

- ....

THE CONVERSATION CONTINUES...

1. What days were special for your family when you were a child?

2. Which relative do you feel closest to?

3. What makes that relationship special?

4. Whom do you respect the most in your family? Why?

5. Does your family hold reunions? Can you describe a recent one?

6. How do you keep in touch with distant relatives? Do you use email?

7. How many times has your family moved? Why?

8. Could you describe some of your favorite family photographs?

9. Is divorce legal in Vietnam? Are there particular conditions required for divorce? What are they? Any other restrictions?

10. What might cause someone to become a "black sheep" in a family?

11. What things might parents keep secret from their children?

12. What things might children keep secret from their parents?

13. Do you have any step or half brothers or sisters? Do you think these relationships are harder? Why?

14. What rivalries has your family had? Have you felt any rivalry with relatives?

15. How can families create stress?

16. What were some important events in your family history?

17. Which ancestor would you most like to meet? Why?

18. How are family habits and traditions different in the United States than in Vietnam?

19. How can people build stronger and healthier family relationships?

20. What do you love most about your family?

DISCUSSING QUOTATIONS

Take turns reading these quotations out loud, and discuss them with your partner. Do you agree with the quotation? Disagree? Why? Mark your answer.

1. "All happy families resemble one another; every unhappy family is unhappy in its own fashion."
   —Leo Tolstoy (1828–1910), Russian novelist

   ☐ Agree ☐ Disagree Why? ....

2. "We never know the love of a parent until we become parents ourselves."
   —Henry Ward Beecher (1813–1887), American speaker

   ☐ Agree ☐ Disagree Why? ....

3. "Rearing a family is probably the most difficult job in the world."
   —Virginia Satir (1916–1988), family therapist

   ☐ Agree ☐ Disagree Why? ....

4. "There are fathers who do not love their children; there is no grandfather who does not adore his grandson."
   —Victor Hugo (1802-1885), French novelist

   ☐ Agree ☐ Disagree Why? ....

5. "Everyone needs to have access both to grandparents and grandchildren in order to be a full human being."
   —Margaret Mead (1901-1978), American anthropologist

   ☐ Agree ☐ Disagree Why? ....

6. "We must learn to live together as brothers or perish as fools."
   —Dr. Martin Luther King, Jr. (1929–1968), civil rights leader, Nobel Prize winner (1964)

   ☐ Agree ☐ Disagree Why? ....

7. "When you are a mother, you're never really alone in your thoughts. A mother always has to think twice, once for herself and once for her child."
   —Sophia Loren (1934–), Italian actress

   ☐ Agree ☐ Disagree Why? ....

8. "There can be no situation in life in which the conversation of my dear sister will not administer some comfort to me."
   —Mary Montagu (1689-1762), English writer

   ☐ Agree ☐ Disagree Why? ....

9. "A sister can be seen as someone who is both ourselves and very much not ourselves - a special kind of double."
   —Toni Morrison (1931-), American Nobel Prize winning novelist

   ☐ Agree ☐ Disagree Why? ....

10. "In every conceivable manner, the family is the link to our past, and the bridge to our future."
    —Alex Haley (1921-1992), American novelist

    ☐ Agree ☐ Disagree Why? ....

⭐ ON YOUR OWN

List your parents, grandparents and children. Give birth dates if they are known and death dates if a person is deceased. Prepare to share with your class partners. Take it one step further, and create a family tree!

....
....
....
....
....
....
....
....
....
....
....
....
....
....
....
....
....

Chapter Notes

CHAPTER 5
EATING AND DRINKING

SHARING TASTES

Everybody eats. Food is both a necessity and a pleasure, and remains a safe and interesting way to learn more about people. Interview your partner and share your eating and drinking experiences.

1. Do you consider eating a chore, a duty, or a pleasure? Why?

2. What did you eat yesterday? Was it a typical day?

3. Do you drink juice/tea/coffee in the morning? Regular or decaffeinated?

4. Do you eat at the same time each day? Or do you eat when you have time?

5. Do you prefer salty snacks or sweet snacks? How often do you snack?

6. Where do you usually shop for food? What shopping tips can you share?

7. What drinks do you often have with your evening meal?

8. What kind of meat do you enjoy eating? Beef? Pork? Poultry? Fish?

9. What is your favorite vegetable? Are you a vegetarian?

10. What is your favorite fruit? Which fruits do you find delicious?

11. Can you name three American dishes that you really enjoy or savor?

12. Which Vietnamese dishes would you recommend to a tourist? Why?

13. Which regional foods in Vietnam do you like the most? What are they?

EXPANDING VOCABULARY

chef	culinary	decaffeinated	edible	famine
fast	feast	gluttony	savor	vegetarian

chef *noun*: a professional cook; the head cook in a restaurant.

• The chef's specialty was broiled fish and his tasty seafood stew.

culinary *noun*: having to do with cooking and food; concerning superior preparation of food.

• Study the culinary arts if you want to become a chef.

decaffeinated *adjective*: containing no caffeine; a drink with the caffeine removed.

• Sue drank decaffeinated coffee because regular coffee made her nervous.

edible *adjective*: something that can be eaten.

• Hungry people know insects are edible during famines.

famine *noun*: an extreme scarcity of edible food.

> **"Gluttony is not a secret vice."**
>
> —Orson Welles (1915-1985), great director/actor

• The terrible famine caused deep suffering and thousands of deaths.

fast *adverb*: moving with speed, advancing or progressing rapidly;
noun: a period of time without eating; verb to go without eating.

• Thang's motorbike can go very fast, but it goes slow in city traffic.

• The word "breakfast" literally means to break the fast.

• Some people fast on holidays and some people fast to lose weight.

feast *noun*: a large, excellent meal; an abundant amount of well-prepared food.

• My mother prepared a feast to celebrate my graduation.

gluttony *noun*: an excess of eating or drinking; greedy or excessive indulgence.

• Gluttony is a common problem among overweight Americans.

savor *verb*: to really enjoy; to experience satisfaction and pleasure in taste or smell.

• Eat slowly to savor this fabulous dinner that my grandmother prepared.

vegetarian *noun*: one who eats no meat; a no-meat diet.

• As a vegetarian, Sari doesn't eat meat.

ASKING QUESTIONS

A. Select five vocabulary words in this chapter, and write a question for each word. Remember to start your question with a question word (Who, What, Where, When, Why, How, Is, Are, Do, Did, Does, etc). You also want to end each question with a question mark (?). Underline each vocabulary word.

Example: Do you know the restaurant's chef?

1...

2...

3...

4...

5. ....

B. Take turns asking and answering questions with your partner or group members.

IDIOMS, PUNS, AND PROVERBS

We have many expressions about food, and some word jokes. Read the following expressions, and discuss them with your partner. What do they mean? Circle your favorites. Explain your choices.

- Hunger finds no fault with the meal.

- One must eat to live, not live to eat.—Spanish

- Many dishes make many dishes.—Vietnamese

- Eat with regimen, drink with measure.—Vietnamese

- I'm on a seafood diet. I see food and I eat it.—American

- She loves ice cream and cookies. She has a sweet tooth.—American

- A boiled egg in the morning is hard to beat.—American

- Eat, drink, and be merry.—English

- The most sincere love is the love of food.—French

- Gluttons dig their grave with their teeth.—English

THE CONVERSATION CONTINUES...

1. What is your favorite restaurant? In what language do you order?

2. How often do you eat at a fast food restaurant? Why?

3. Are American fast food chains popular in Vietnam? Why?

4. Did all members of your family eat the evening meal together? Who cooked the food? Who served the food?

5. In Vietnam, what foods or drinks are associated with weddings? Birthdays? Funerals?

6. What foods or drinks are associated with holy days or national holidays?

7. Have you ever eaten at a feast? When? What meals remind you of happy times?

8. Have you ever fasted? Why? Were you famished after skipping two meals?

9. Does your religion have dietary rules or restrictions? What are they?

10. Has there ever been a famine in Vietnam? What caused it?

11. Have you ever tried to diet to lose weight? What did you do?

12. Can you name several types of diets?

13. Is your diet restricted in any way by health considerations? How?

14. Do you ever read food labels? Do you have any food allergies?

15. What meals does your family share? Who cooks? Who serves?

16. Does your family share recipes? Which recipe would you like?

17. Would you like to share a favorite recipe?

18. Are you adventurous in seeking out new culinary delights?

19. What is your ideal dinner? Describe the dishes, guests, and location.

★ NOTES & QUOTES

....

....

....

....

....

....

....

....

DISCUSSING QUOTATIONS

Take turns reading these quotations out loud, and discuss them with your partner. Do you agree with the quotation? Disagree? Why? Mark your answer.

1. "Better beans and bacon in peace than cakes and ale in fear."
   —Aesop (ca. 550 B.C.)

   ☐ Agree ☐ Disagree Why? ....

2. "The satiated man and the hungry one do not see the same thing when they look upon a loaf of bread."
   —Rumi (1207–1273), Persian poet and mystic

   ☐ Agree ☐ Disagree Why? ....

3. "If it's beautifully arranged on the plate, you know someone's fingers have been all over it."
   —Julia Child (1912–2004), American chef/author

   ☐ Agree ☐ Disagree Why? ....

4. "Live. Love. Eat."
   —Wolfgang Puck (1949–), chef

   ☐ Agree ☐ Disagree Why? ....

5. "When I drink, I think; and when I think, I drink."
   —Francois Rabelais (1495–1553), satirist

6. "Edible (adj). Good to eat and wholesome to digest, as a worm to a toad, a toad to a snake, a snake to a pig, a pig to a man, and a man to a worm."
   —Ambrose Bierce (1842–1916), American writer

   ☐ Agree ☐ Disagree Why? ....

7. "The secret of staying young is to live honestly, eat slowly, and lie about your age."
   —Lucille Desiree Ball (1911–1984), American TV star and actress

   ☐ Agree ☐ Disagree Why? ....

8. "People who drink to drown their sorrow should be told that sorrow knows how to swim."
   —Ann Landers (1918–2002), American advice columnist

   ☐ Agree ☐ Disagree Why? ....

9. "I thought, I called, I planned, I shopped, I schlepped, I cleaned, I chopped, I soaked, I peeled, I rinsed, I grated, I minced, I simmered, I larded, I mixed, I fried, I boiled, I baked, I sauteed, I souffleed, I flame broiled, and I sweated. So, tell me it's great!"
   —Slogan on a novelty kitchen apron in the United States

   ☐ Agree ☐ Disagree Why? ....

10. "More die in the United States of too much food than of too little."
    —John Kenneth Galbraith (1908–2006) ambassador, economist

    ☐ Agree ☐ Disagree Why? ....

⭐ ON YOUR OWN

Write menu descriptions for your perfect meal. Include the major ingredients of dishes as one finds on a menu.

Be sure to include appetizers, beverages and desserts. Indulge yourself. Now describe your delicious choices to your group.

....

....

....

....

....

....

Role Playing a Night Out at a Fancy Restaurant

ROLE PLAY PREPARATION: ASKING QUESTIONS

Eating out can be fun and satisfying, especially if ordering in English.

What are three typical questions to ask a waiter at a nice restaurant?

1...

2...

3...

What are three questions you might ask a friend at dinner?

1...

2...

3...

ROLE PLAY: ACCIDENTS HAPPEN!

Everybody wants to have a good time when they go out, but sometimes bad things happen to good people—even in nice restaurants!

Let's imagine this situation: Two friends are going to dinner, and they want to talk. At the restaurant, a new waiter has just started. He's very nervous. It's a busy night at a fashionable restaurant on Saturday night. Everybody wants to have a good time, but accidents do happen.

What will happen? ....

Who are the friends? ....

What do they want to talk about? ....

What's the restaurant's name?..

Where is the restaurant? ....

Who is the waiter? ....

Why is the restaurant so busy?...

What accidents will happen?...

What will happen next?...

Can you create a fun skit? Answer the questions and act in your own play. Have fun.

Chapter Notes

CHAPTER 6
EXPLORING DAILY HABITS

SHARING STORIES

Do you know your own habits? Share stories about your habits and find out more about your partner's habits in a friendly exchange.

1. How many hours of sleep do you usually get? Is that enough sleep for you?

2. What time do you usually get up in the morning? Do you get up with the sun?

3. Do you jump out of bed? Are you a "morning monster"?

4. Can you describe your morning habits? Are you in a hurry?

5. What do you eat for breakfast? What do you prefer to drink in the morning?

6. Can you describe a typical summer afternoon for you? A winter afternoon?

7. How did you come to school today? Did you arrive by foot, by bus, by car or by bike?

8. How long is your daily commute to work or school?

9. What's your daily schedule like? Busy? Slow? Loose? Full?

10. What was your daily schedule like five years ago? How is different now?

11. Do you do many things at the last minute? Why?

12. In your daily life, what modern appliances or machines do you use?

13. What task or chore have you put off or postponed?

14. Where do you prefer to shop for clothes? Why?

15. Do you like to bargain while shopping? Why?

16. Where do you like buying your groceries? Why?

17. What do you usually buy at the market?

EXPANDING VOCABULARY

bargain	consumer	curious	discipline	habit
impulsive	lifestyle	oversleep	routine	schedule

bargain *noun*: a good buy for the price; *verb*: to try to buy an item at a cheaper price.

• I like to shop for bargains in the markets, and often I bargain with sellers.

consumer *noun*: a person who buys products or services.

• Consumers like bargains where they can buy quality products at low prices.

> "We are what we repeatedly do. Excellence, then, is not an act, but a habit."—Aristotle (384 -322 B.C.E), Ancient Greek philosopher

curious *adjective*: an active desire to learn or know about things; strange or unusual.

• I am curious about your educational programs.

• Jill had a curious habit of stroking her eyebrow when she talked to me.

disciplined *adjective*: following a strict routine.

• You need a more disciplined approach to learn more and get better grades.

habit *noun*: repeated course of action developed over time; settled routine;

• By habit and self-discipline, he got up before dawn and worked until sunset.

impulsive *adjective*: to suddenly act.

• Kara was impulsive, and bought the expensive, new motorbike without telling her parents or knowing how to pay for gas.

lifestyle *noun:* the way a person leads their life.

• He kept a simple lifestyle: he ate healthy food, worked hard six days a week, and read poetry at night.

oversleep *verb*: to sleep late; to fail to wake up on time.

• I set two alarm clocks to be sure I wouldn't oversleep and miss my final examination at school.

routine *noun*: the same activity or pattern; established way of acting;

adjective: usual, typical

• My mother follows the same routine everyday—she wakes up at 5 in the morning and goes to sleep at 10 at night.

• The routine medical check-up confirmed the patient's good health.

schedule *noun*: a timetable or a series of events; *verb*: to make appointments.

• My schedule is full. Can we meet next week?

• I will schedule you with the doctor on Tuesday at 3.

ASKING QUESTIONS

A. Select five vocabulary words in this chapter, and write a question for each word. Remember to start your question with a question word (Who, What, Where, When, Why, How, Is, Are, Do, Did, Does, etc). You also want to end each question with a question mark (?). Underline each vocabulary word.

Example: What is your schedule for next semester?

1. ....

2. ....

3. ....

4. ....

5. ....

B. Take turns asking and answering questions with your partner or group members.

⭐ **ON YOUR OWN**

Write down your schedule for one day. Remember to include meals and meetings. Share your schedule with your conversation partner.

7 a.m. ....

8 ....

9 ....

10 ....

11 ....

12 ....

1 ....

2 ....

3 ....

4 ....

5 ....

6 ....

7 p.m. ....

PARAPHRASING PROVERBS

A. Read the following proverbs, and discuss them with your partner. What do they mean? Circle your favorites. Explain your choices.

- Doing nothing is doing ill.—Vietnamese

- The more you chew your meat, the better it tastes; The more you speak, the lighter your heart becomes.—Korean

- An old cat will never learn to dance.—Moroccan

- Habits are first cobwebs, then cables.—Spanish

- Love makes marriage possible, and habit makes it endurable.—American

- The fool in a hurry drinks his tea with chopsticks.—Chinese

- Precaution brings no worries.—Vietnamese

B. Can you add two more?

....

....

THE CONVERSATION CONTINUES...

1. Do you look for bargains when shopping? Are you a bargain hunter?

2. What are your TV viewing habits? Do you always watch certain shows? Which ones?

3. How often do you use a computer? When do you send email?

4. Do you find daily life in a big city hectic? Can you give some examples?

5. What are some dangerous or unhealthy habits?

6. Do you consider smoking a bad habit? Why?

7. In what ways are you self-disciplined?

8. Are you sometimes lazy? How?

9. Do you tend to see the glass as half-full or half-empty? Are you more of an optimist or a pessimist? Why?

10. What is your favorite time of day? Why?

11. What are some of your healthier habits?

12. What are some of your less healthy habits?

13. How do your habits compare to your parents' habits at your age?

14. Have your daily habits changed in the last five years? How?

15. Given a choice, would you prefer to live now or 100 years ago? Why?

 **REMEMBER...**

- Work hard.

- Reflect.

- Choose wisely.

✪ ON YOUR OWN

Keep an activity log for a day. Share it with your conversation partner.

1 ....
2 ....
3 ....
4 ....
5 ....
6 ....
7 ....
8 ....
9 ....
10 ....

DISCUSSING QUOTATIONS

Take turns reading these quotations out loud, and discuss them with your partner. Do you agree with the quotation? Disagree? Why? Mark your answer.

1. "Nothing is in reality either pleasant or unpleasant by nature; but all things become so through habit."
   —Epictetus (55–135), Greek stoic philosopher

   ☐ Agree ☐ Disagree Why? ....

2. "Men's natures are alike; it is their habits that separate them."
   —Confucius (551–479 B.C.E.) great Chinese philosopher

   ☐ Agree ☐ Disagree Why? ....

3. "We are what we repeatedly do. Excellence, then, is not an act, but a habit."
   —Aristotle (384–322 B.C.E.), Ancient Greek philosopher

   ☐ Agree ☐ Disagree Why? ....

4. "Nothing so needs reforming as other people's habits."
   —Mark Twain (1835–1910), American writer/humorist

   ☐ Agree ☐ Disagree Why? ....

5. "Habit for him was all the test of truth; 'It must be right: I've done it from my youth.'"
   —George Crabbe (1754–1832), English poet

   ☐ Agree ☐ Disagree Why? ....

6. "The perpetual obstacle to human advancement is custom."
   —John Stuart Mill (1806–1873), English political philosopher

   ☐ Agree ☐ Disagree Why? ....

7. "The chains of habit are too weak to be felt until they are too strong to be broken."
   —Dr. Samuel Johnson (1709–1784), English author

   ☐ Agree ☐ Disagree Why? ....

8. "Any man who reads too much and uses his own brain too little falls into lazy habits of thinking."
   —Albert Einstein (1879–1955), physicist, Nobel Prize winner (1921) and *Time* magazine's Man of the 20th Century

   ☐ Agree ☐ Disagree Why? ....

9. "For many, negative thinking is a habit, which over time, becomes an addiction."
   —Peter McWilliams (1949–2000), American self-help author

   ☐ Agree ☐ Disagree Why? ....

10. "The unfortunate thing about this world is that good habits are so much easier to give up than bad ones."
    —Somerset Maugham (1874–1965), English novelist

    ☐ Agree ☐ Disagree Why? ....

Chapter Notes

....
....
....
....
....
....
....
....
....
....
....
....
....
....
....
....
....
....
....
....
....
....
....
....
....

CHAPTER 7
BEING YOURSELF

SHARING PERSPECTIVES

From consulting charts and reading palms to taking personality tests and reading self-help books, people love to describe themselves.

1. Which three adjectives would you use to describe your personality?

2. Are you shy or outgoing? When are you most outgoing?

3. Are you daring or cautious? In what ways?

4. Are you usually patient or impatient? Can you give an example?

5. Are you quiet or talkative? When are you most talkative? Least?

6. Would you call yourself a leader or a follower? Why?

7. Are you generous or selfish? Are you too selfish or overly generous?

8. In what ways are you rigid? In what ways are you flexible?

9. In what ways are you traditional? In what ways are you modern?

10. If pessimistic is 1 and optimistic is 10, what would your number be on the scale? Why did you decide on that number?

11. On a scale of 1-10, how assertive are you?

12. Is your personality more like your mother or your father? In what ways?

13. Which color would you use to describe your personality?

14. Which animal would you use to describe yourself? Tiger? Mouse? Why?

15. Do you believe in astrology? Which sign are you in the zodiac? Does the pattern of this sign match your personality?

16. Which animal year are you according to Chinese astrology? Does this fit?

17. Have you ever taken a personality test from a magazine or online? Was it helpful? Was it fun? Was it accurate?

18. Which season of the year best describes your personality? In what ways?

EXPANDING VOCABULARY

accurate	character	flexible	generous	nurture
patient	optimist	pessimist	rigid	talkative

accurate *adjective*: correct, getting the facts right.

• Scientists, engineers, and doctors must be accurate.

"Character is much easier kept than recovered."

—Thomas Paine (1737-1809), American revolutionary

character *noun*: one's personality and values; moral sense; a figure in fiction or theater.

- Kelly showed her character at work.
- Oliver Twist is one of my favorite characters in English literature.

flexible *adjective*: loose, bending; willing to change.

- Pham is flexible and can work either Friday or Saturday.

generous: *adjective*: giving, sharing with others.

- A good sister is generous with her time and helps her family.

nurture *verb*: to take care of another; to care for or help someone in need.

- Parents nurture their children and guide them in their lives.

patient *adjective*: able to wait calmly, not in a hurry;

noun: a person receiving medical treatment.

- A patient man can calmly wait for a late bus.
- The doctor prescribed medicine for her patient.

optimist *noun*: someone who see the positive side and believes things will get better.

- She saw the glass as "half-full," which made her an optimist.

pessimist *noun*: one who has a negative view, and thinks things will get worse.

- He saw the glass as "half-empty," which made him a pessimist.

rigid *adjective*: unwilling to change; inflexible.

- Thomas is so rigid that he will not even listen to other people.

talkative *adjective*: verbal; engages in constant or non-stop conversation.

- Tran becomes talkative when he relaxes with his friends.

ASKING QUESTIONS

A. Select five vocabulary words in this chapter, and write a question for each word. Remember to start your question with a question word (Who, What, When, Where, Why, How, Is, Do, etc). You also want to end each question with a question mark (?). Underline each vocabulary word.

Example: Are you feeling optimistic today?

1..

2..

3..

4..

5..

B. Take turns asking and answering questions with your partner or group members.

⭐ **REMEMBER...**

- Respect yourself
- Be yourself
- Create your future

PARAPHRASING PROVERBS

A. Read the following proverbs, and discuss them with your partner. What do they mean? Circle your favorites. Explain your choices.

- Character is destiny.—Greek

- The leopard can not change its spots.—Vietnamese

- Trust yourself.—American

- The more noble, the more humble.—Chinese

- A light heart lives long.—English

- See yourself as others see you.

- A pretty being is better than being pretty.—English

B. Can you add two more?

- ....

- ....

THE CONVERSATION CONTINUES...

1. Do you think our personalities are set when we are born?

2. Can we change our personalities? How?

3. How has your personality changed in the last ten years?

4. Which three words would you use to describe your best friend's personality?

5. How are your personalities similar? How are your personalities different?

6. Why do you think opposites are sometimes attracted to each other?

7. Some cultures define personality in terms of the elements. Would you say you are primarily air, water, fire, or earth? Explain your choice.

8. Which three qualities do you think of as yin (feminine)?

9. Which three qualities do you think of as yang (masculine)?

10. Can you name one yin quality and one yang quality which describe you?

11. How might being raised in poverty influence someone's personality?

12. Would being born in extreme wealth change your personality? How?

13. If you had been born in another country, do you think your personality would be different? How?

14. Can you think of somebody with a good personality and bad character?

15. What is the difference between one's personality and one's character?

16. Are you primarily an extrovert or an introvert? Why do you say that?

17. Do you think nature (biology) or nurture (our circumstances) are more important in shaping our personalities? Why do you say that?

18. What are your best qualities?

36

DISCUSSING QUOTATIONS

Take turns reading these quotations out loud, and discuss them with your partner. Do you agree with the quotation? Disagree? Why? Mark your answer.

1. "Know thyself."
   —Socrates (470-399 B.C.E.), Greek philosopher

   ☐ Agree ☐ Disagree Why? ....

2. "The man of character bears the accidents of life with dignity and grace, making the best of circumstances."
   —Aristotle (384–322 B.C.E.), Greek philosopher/ethicist

   ☐ Agree ☐ Disagree Why? ....

3. "This above all: To thine own self be true, And it must follow, as the night the day, Thou canst not then be false to any man."
   —William Shakespeare (1564-1616), English playwright

   ☐ Agree ☐ Disagree Why? ....

4. "Character is much easier kept than recovered."
   —Thomas Paine (1737–1809), American writer

   ☐ Agree ☐ Disagree Why? ....

5. "It is absurd to divide people into good and bad. People are either charming or tedious."
   —Oscar Wilde (1856–1900), Irish author/playwright

   ☐ Agree ☐ Disagree Why? ....

6. "Some people with great virtues are disagreeable, while others with great vice are delightful."
   —Francois de la Rochefoucauld (1613—1680), French philosopher

   ☐ Agree ☐ Disagree Why? ....

7. "Man's main task in life is to give birth to himself, to become what he potentially is. The most important product of his effort is his own personality."
   —Erich Fromm (1900–1980), German-American psychologist

   ☐ Agree ☐ Disagree Why? ....

8. "Generous people are rarely mentally ill people."
   —Karl Menninger (1893–1990), American psychiatrist

   ☐ Agree ☐ Disagree Why? ....

9. "The easiest kind of relationship for me is with ten thousand people. The hardest is with one."
   —Joan Baez (1941 -), American singer

   ☐ Agree ☐ Disagree Why? ....

10. "Dwell in possibility."
    —Emily Dickinson (1830-1886), American poet

    ☐ Agree ☐ Disagree Why? ....

⭐ ON YOUR OWN

What do you like about yourself? Write a postcard to a friend describing your strongest traits.

....
....
....
....
....
....
....
....
....
....

Chapter Notes

CHAPTER 8
STAYING HEALTHY

WALKING THE WALK

Sometimes it is easier to talk the talk about staying healthy than walking the walk to stay healthy. Interview your partner and exchange health tips.

1. What are some signs of being healthy?

2. What do your friends or relatives do to stay healthy?

3. What do you do to stay healthy?

4. Have your health habits changed in the last few years? How?

5. What is something that many people should do, but don't do to stay healthy?

6. Do you know any home remedies for common ailments?

7. How do you treat a sore throat? Minor cut? Headaches?

8. What are some causes of back pain? What are some remedies?

9. Do you take daily vitamins? Which ones? Why?

10. Do you regularly take over-the-counter drugs or prescription drugs? Why?

11. How often do you wash your hands? What other precautions do you take to prevent the spread of germs?

12. Do you eat healthy food? Do you have any unhealthy eating habits?

13. Do you enjoy smoking? What are some of the dangers of smoking?

14. How much sleep do you usually get? Is your sleep restful, or do you toss and turn?

15. How often do you feel tired or exhausted? What can you do to feel more energetic?

EXPANDING VOCABULARY

exercise	germ	medication	operation	overcome
prescription	prevent	prevention	remedy	symptom

exercise *noun*: physical activity to maintain good health;

verb: to be physically active; to perform activities well.

• I get my daily exercise by bicycling to work.

• Le exercises good judgment and seldom makes mistakes.

germ *noun*: a tiny organism that can cause illness, such as a virus or bacteria.

• Germs in undercooked food can cause you to get sick.

If one has no illness, he is already rich.

—Korean proverb

medication *noun*: a pill or other treatment designed to cure an illness.

• If he won't take his medication, his condition will probably get worse.

operation *noun*: surgery; a medical procedure that cuts into and opens up the body; a company or business action.

• It took Hong six weeks to recover from the medical operation performed by his doctor.

• Chin manages the department and runs the entire operation, beginning to end.

overcome *verb*: to achieve your goals despite having to face difficult challenges along the way.

• "We shall overcome" was the slogan of Dr. Martin Luther King, the famous African-American civil rights leader and Nobel Prize winner.

prescription *noun*: a written form signed by a doctor authorizing the purchase of medicine.

• Dr. Tam wrote the prescription so the patient could get his medicine.

prevent *verb*: to stop something from taking place, to keep it from happening.

• Hank took his medicine for 10 days to prevent his illness from returning.

prevention *noun*: stopping something from happening

• "Prevention is better than medication" is a nursing proverb.

remedy *noun*: a medicine or treatment that relieves or cures a disease or symptom; *verb*: to cure.

• Aspirin is a common remedy for headaches, but other remedies exist, too.

symptom *noun*: a sign of a disease or disorder; visible proof some other problem exists.

• The doctor recognized the fever and cough as classic flu symptoms.

ASKING QUESTIONS

A. Select five vocabulary words in this chapter, and write a question for each word. Remember to start your question with a question word (Who, What, When, Where, Why, How, Is, Do, etc). You also want to end each question with a question mark (?). Underline each vocabulary word.

Example: How often do you exercise?

1..

2..

3..

4..

5..

B. Take turns asking and answering questions with your partner or group members.

⭐ **ON YOUR OWN**

List your top five tips for staying healthy and happy. Prepare to share your advice with the class.

1..
....

2..
....

3..
....

4..
....

5..
....

PARAPHRASING PROVERBS

A. Read the following proverbs, and discuss them with your partner. What do they mean? Circle your favorites. Explain your choices.

• Health is a jewel.—Vietnamese

• An apple a day keeps the doctor away.—English

• A sick person is a prisoner.—Yemenite

• He who has health has hope, and he who has hope, has everything.—Arabian

• Nature, time, and patience are the three great physicians.—Irish

• Prevention beats medication.— Dutch

• Moderation is the mother of good health.— Canadian

• Old age is a thousand headaches.—Persian

B. Can you add two more?

• ....

• ....

THE CONVERSATION CONTINUES...

1. Do you exercise regularly? What are your favorite exercises?

2. Do you take regular walks? Ride a bike? Gather in a park to exercise? Go swimming or practice Tai-chi?

3. What can cause stomach aches? Do you eat quickly? Do you eat spicy foods?

4. Do you find yourself worrying a lot? Do you have ulcers?

5. What are some public health issues in Vietnam?

6. What are some common diseases in Asia today?

7. Have you ever been to a hospital? Why? What made it memorable?

8. Are you at your ideal weight? Should you gain weight to attain your ideal? Should you lose weight to attain your ideal?

9. Do you restrict your diet for health reasons? How? Why?

10. Do our emotions and thoughts affect our health? How?

11. What three things could you do to improve your general health?

12. How has medicine improved over the last 100 years?

13. What are some advantages of watching your health?

14. What advice can you give me to stay healthy?

15. How can we help our friends stay healthy?

DISCUSSING QUOTATIONS

Take turns reading these quotations out loud, and discuss them with your partner. Do you agree with the quotation? Disagree? Why? Mark your answer.

1. "The secret of health for both mind and body is not to mourn for the past, not to worry about the future, not to anticipate troubles, but to live in the present moment wisely and earnestly."
   —Siddhartha Guatama (563–483 B.C.), Buddha, spiritual leader

   ☐ Agree ☐ Disagree Why? ....

2. "The first duty of a physician is that he should do the sick no harm."
   —Hippocrates (460–380 B.C.), ancient Greek physician

   ☐ Agree ☐ Disagree Why? ....

3. "It is part of the cure to wish to be cured."
   —Seneca the Younger (4 B.C.–65 A.D.), Roman philosopher/statesmen

   ☐ Agree ☐ Disagree Why? ....

4. "Better use medicines at the outset than at the last moment."
   —Publilius Syrus (85–43 B.C.E.), Roman writer

   ☐ Agree ☐ Disagree Why? ....

5. "A sound mind in a sound body is a short, but full description of a happy state in this world."
   —John Locke (1632–1704), English philosopher

   ☐ Agree ☐ Disagree Why? ....

6. "Early to bed and early to rise makes a man healthy, wealthy, and wise."
   —Benjamin Franklin (1706–1790), American writer/publisher

   ☐ Agree ☐ Disagree Why? ....

7. "You can't lose weight by talking about it. You have to keep your mouth shut."
   —Benjamin Franklin (1706-1790), American writer/publisher

   ☐ Agree ☐ Disagree Why? ....

8. "You can't ignore the importance of a good digestion. The joy of life… depends on a sound stomach."
   —Joseph Conrad (1857–1924), Polish-born English author

   ☐ Agree ☐ Disagree Why? ....

9. "The only way to keep your health is to eat what you don't want, drink what you don't like, and do what you'd rather not."
   —Mark Twain (1835–1910), American writer/humorist

   ☐ Agree ☐ Disagree Why? ....

10. "Be careful about reading a health book. You may die of a misprint."
    —Mark Twain (1835–1910), American writer/humorist

    ☐ Agree ☐ Disagree Why? ....

42   **www.CompellingConversations.com**

Getting Health Advice from the Internet

Student Name .... Class ....

Teacher: .... Date ....

Everybody wants to stay healthy, but many people make unhealthy lifestyle choices. Select a video that gives advice on how to stay healthy—in English—that you would like to share with your classmates. Watch the video, take notes, and summarize the health advice for your classmates.

1. Video title: ....

2. Web address..

3. Length................. 4. Creator:..

5. Please describe the video: ....

....

....

6. What health tips did the video provide? ....

....

7. Where do you think the video was produced? Why?...

....

8. How practical did you find the health tips? Why? ....

....

9. What was the strongest part? Why?...

....

10. What was the weakest part? Why? ....

....

11. Does the advice seem reliable and trustworthy? Why? ....

....

12. Who do you think is the audience for this video?..

....

13. Why did you choose this video? ....

....

14. How would you rate this video on a scale of 1 to 5 stars? Why? ....

....

Chapter Notes

CHAPTER 9
BEING A CHILD—AND BECOMING A PARENT

SHARING EXPERIENCES

Everyone was once a child; most people are or will become parents. Share your experiences and exchange ideas on the pleasures and challenges of being a child and a parent.

1. Where are you in your family's birth order?

2. How old were your parents when you were born?

3. Did your parents ever live with their parents?

4. When you were a baby, who was your primary caretaker?

5. What activities do you remember doing with your mother?

6. What activities do you remember doing with your father?

7. Do you remember playing with your parents? What did you play?

8. When you were a child, were you ever punished? How? Why?

9. Which of your parents was the main disciplinarian in your family?

10. Were the rules different for girls than for boys? What about family expectations for girls and boys?

11. Do you remember helping either of your parents with chores? Which ones?

12. When might parents hover over their children?

13. What did your parents expect from you as a teenager? Did you rebel?

14. Which parenting duties do you think your parents did well?

15. What would you like to change about the way your parents treated you as a child? A teenager? Why?

16. Are you close with your father or mother now? What do you do together?

17. Do you resemble either of your parents? How?

18. What are you grateful to your parents for?

EXPANDING VOCABULARY

chores	duty	ideal	loyal	primary
protect	qualities	resemble	sacrifice	spank

chores *noun*: small helpful tasks; a routine, daily job to do.

• Hannah's daily chores included clearing the table and washing the dishes.

> "When I was a boy of fourteen, my father was so ignorant I could hardly stand to have the old man around. But when I got be twenty-one, I was astonished at how much he had learned in seven years."
>
> —Mark Twain (1835-1910), American humorist

duty *noun*: A task or chore that a person is expected to perform.

• It was the nurse's duty to watch the patient until he awoke from his coma.

ideal *noun*: a standard of excellence, beauty or perfection; the best possible result in a situation; *adjective*: perfect, absolute, without fault.

• Racial equality is a noble ideal.

• Trang was his ideal woman: she was intelligent, beautiful, and loyal.

loyal *adjective*: faithful to a person, thing, or government; demonstrating commitment to others.

• She was loyal to her family and never forgot her poorer, rural relatives.

primary *adjective*: the one thing ranked as the most important;

• My primary reason to buy a motorcycle is to reduce my commute to work.

protect *verb*: to prevent personal harm; to guard against damage or destruction from others..

• Protect yourself and wear a helmet while driving a motorbike.

quality *noun*: noteworthy feature or personal trait; the essential character of excellence.

• His best qualities were his dedication, sense of humor, and honesty.

resemble *noun*: look like, be similar to something else.

• Ahn resembles her father more than her mother.

sacrifice *verb*: to give up something valuable; to suffer a personal loss to realize a greater good;

• Paul sacrificed his health in order to work in the mine and feed his family.

spank *verb*: to hit on the bottom, usually as punishment of a child.

• Spanking is a common punishment of children in many countries, but it is illegal in California.

ASKING QUESTIONS

A. Select five vocabulary words in this chapter, and write a question for each word. Remember to start your question with a question word (Who, What, Where, Why, Are, Is, Do, If, Whether, etc). You also want to end each question with a question mark (?). Underline each vocabulary word.

Example: How do parents encourage their children?

1...

2...

3...

4...

5...

B. Take turns asking and answering questions with your partner or group members.

PARAPHRASING PROVERBS

A. Read the following proverbs, and discuss them with your partner. What do they mean? Circle your favorites. Explain your choices.

- Love your children with your heart, but train them with your hands.—Ukrainian

- Don't threaten a child; either punish him or forgive him.

- It's an ill bird that fouls its own nest.—Chinese

- Emeralds and crystals glitter when lit.—Japanese

- Blood is thicker than water.

- Obeying from love is better than obeying from fear.

- We are all Uncle Ho's children.—Vietnamese

- When the father's generation eats salt, the child's generation thirsts for water.—Vietnamese

B. Can you add two more?

- ....

- ....

THE CONVERSATION CONTINUES...

1. Are you especially close with any of your siblings? What do you do together?

2. Do you have children? What are their ages?

3. Can you briefly describe each of your children?

4. Do you want children? How many?

5. In what ways do you hope to repeat the parenting skills of your father and mother? How would you describe their parenting style?

6. Are there ways you hope to be a better parent than your parents? How?

7. When, if ever, do you discipline your children? What are some methods of discipline? Talking? Additional chores? Grounding? Spanking? What works best?

8. How do parents sacrifice for their children? Why isn't this always appreciated?

9. What do you think is the ideal age for parents to be? Why?

10. How was it easier to be a parent 40 years ago? How was it more difficult?

11. What are some problems that parents face today?

12. What are some "good mistakes" that parents sometimes make?

13. What are some of the satisfactions of being a parent?

14. What movies have touched you by their depiction of parents and children?

15. How would you describe an ideal father? Ideal mother?

16. What five qualities would you like your children to have?

17. Can you share your top five tips for being a loving parent?

Take turns reading these quotations out loud, and discuss them with your partner. Do you agree with the quotation? Disagree? Why? Mark your answer.

1. "Children today are tyrants. They contradict their parents, gobble their food, and tyrannize their teachers."
   —Socrates (469–399 B.C.E.), Greek philosopher

   ☐ Agree ☐ Disagree Why? ....

2. "A child is not a vase to be filled, but a fire to be lit."
   —Rabelais (1494–1553) French essayist and humanist

   ☐ Agree ☐ Disagree Why? ....

3. "The first half of our lives is ruined by our parents, and the second half by our children."
   —Clarence Darrow (1857–1938), American lawyer

   ☐ Agree ☐ Disagree Why?

4. "No two children are ever born into the same family."
   —Leo Rosten (1908–1997), American writer

   ☐ Agree ☐ Disagree Why? ....

5. "No parent should ever have to choose between work and family; between earning a decent wage and caring for a child."
   —Bill Clinton (1946–), 42nd U.S. President

   ☐ Agree ☐ Disagree Why? ....

6. "In the final analysis, it is not what you do for your children, but what you have taught them to do for themselves that will make them successful human beings."
   —Ann Landers (1918–2002), American advice columnist

   ☐ Agree ☐ Disagree Why?

7. "The only time a woman really succeeds in changing a man is when he's a baby."
   —Natalie Wood (1938-1981), American actress

   ☐ Agree ☐ Disagree Why? ....

8. "Love other human beings as you would love yourself."
   —Ho Chi Minh (1890-1969), Vietnam's first President and statesman

   ☐ Agree ☐ Disagree Why? ....

9. "The family is one of nature's masterpieces."
   —George Santayana (1863-1952), Spanish philosopher

   ☐ Agree ☐ Disagree Why? ....

10. "Rejoice with your family in the beautiful land of life!"
    —Albert Einstein (1879-1955), Nobel Prize winner in Physics

    ☐ Agree ☐ Disagree Why? ....

★ ON YOUR OWN

Interview a successful parent.

What tips does that person offer?

Or. . .list five things you are grateful for.

1..

2. ....

3..

4. ....

5..

chapter Notes

CHAPTER 10
MAKING AND KEEPING FRIENDS

SHARING MEMORIES

We all want good friends. How does one make good friends? Share your ideas about friendship with your partner.

1. Did you have a best friend when you were an 8-year-old? Who?

2. What did you do together? Can you describe your best friend?

3. Who was your best friend when you were 14? What did you do?

4. Are you still friends, or pals, with the best friends of your youth?

5. Why do best friends sometimes drift apart?

6. What are some tips for keeping a friendship strong?

7. Who is your best friend now? How did you meet your best friend?

8. What activities do you do with your friend? What makes this friendship special?

9. What do you and your best friend have in common?

10. How are you and your best friend different?

11. Have you seen the TV show "Friends"? Do you like it? Who is your favorite character?

12. Can you think of a good movie about friendship?

13. In your opinion, are there rules for a friendship?

14. What are some things that a good friend should do?

15. Are there things that a good friend should not do? Like what?

16. Do you think you are a good friend to others? In what ways?

17. Do you think friends should loan each other money? Why or why not?

18. How do you deepen friendships? Can you share five tips for making friends?

19. Which of your friends would make good roommates? Why?

20. Do you have any friends that you would not want as roommates?

EXPANDING VOCABULARY

assist	betray	crisis	depend	dependable
drift	pal	roommate	support	supportive

assist *verb*: to help.

• My friends assisted me in cleaning up.

"When the character of a man is not clear to you, look at his friends."

—Japanese

betray *verb*: to violate a trust; to harm or be disloyal.

• I told Kim my secret because I know she won't betray me.

crisis *noun*: an emergency situation; a critical time which requires decisive action.

• The economic crisis caused many workers to lose their jobs and stores to close.

depend *verb*: count on.

• Children depend on their parents for love, protection, and financial support.

dependable *adjective*: loyal, reliable.

• She is dependable; you can count on her help during this difficult time.

drift apart *verb*: to slowly separate; to grow distant.

• They were friends for years, but they began to drift apart when he moved away for work.

pal *noun*: a good friend; a well-known buddy.

• My pal, Chen, can get us tickets.

roommate *noun*: someone you live with; a person who shares a house or bedroom with you.

• I kept the same roommate each year I was in college.

support *verb*: to give help, to assist, to recommend, to make stronger.

• She supported her best friend during a very hard time.

supportive *adjective*: helpful; encouraging.

• My mother is very supportive of my plans to get a graduate degree, but my uncle would prefer I work in his company.

ASKING QUESTIONS

A. Select five vocabulary words in this chapter, and write a question for each word. Remember to start your question with a question word (Who, What, Where, Why, Are, Is, Do, If, Whether, etc.). You also want to end each question with a question mark (?). Underline each vocabulary word.

Example: How do your friends support you?

1..
2..
3..
4..
5..

B. Take turns asking and answering questions with your partner or group members.

REMEMBER...

• Be active

• Be encouraging

• Show understanding

PARAPHRASING PROVERBS

A. Read the following proverbs, and discuss them with your partner. What do they mean? Circle your favorites. Explain your choices.

- Love all, trust a few, do wrong to none.—Vietnamese

- A friend in need is a friend indeed.—Latin

- Never catch a falling knife or a falling friend.—Scottish

- Do not protect yourself by a fence, but rather by your friends.—Czech

- Do not use a hatchet to remove a fly from your friend's face.—Chinese

- Lend money to a good friend, and you will lose the money as well as your friend.—Korean

- Fate chooses your relatives; you choose your friends.—French

- Your best friend is yourself.—American

- Your best friend won't tell you.—American mouthwash ad

- Friendship is like a knife: without sharpening it will rust.—Egyptian

- Eat the plum, but give back a peach.—Vietnamese

B. Can you add two more proverbs about friends?

- ....

- ....

THINK ABOUT IT...

What are three qualities that you look for in a friend?

1..

2..

3..

Fill in the blanks.

A true friend always:...........................

....

A true friend never...........................

....

Discuss your sentences with your partner.

THE CONVERSATION CONTINUES...

1. Why do fast friends often form in crisis situations?
2. How do you meet new friends? Do you have any tips for making friends?
3. How do you keep in touch with friends?
4. Do you use instant messaging with friends?
5. Have you ever Googled a friend, coworker, or date?
6. Do you think that people of the opposite sex can be friends? Why?
7. Do you know a married couple who are best friends?
8. If so, why do you think that relationship works?
9. Have you ever felt betrayed by a friend? How did you react?
10. Do you think it is fair to judge people by their friends? Why?
11. Do you have a close circle of friends? What unites you?
12. Can one be friends with one's parents? Why or why not?
13. Can one be friends with one's children? Why or why not?
14. Can you think of classic stories about true friendship?
15. Why do friends sometimes drift apart?
16. Can you share some tips for keeping a friendship strong?

DISCUSSING QUOTATIONS

Take turns reading these quotations out loud, and discuss them with your partner. Do you agree with the quotation? Disagree? Why? Mark your answer.

1. "Without friends no one would choose to live, though he had all other goods."
   —Aristotle (384–322 B.C.E.), Greek philosopher

   ☐ Agree ☐ Disagree Why? ....

2. "Have no friends not equal to yourself."
   —Confucius (551–479 B.C.E.), Chinese philosopher

   ☐ Agree ☐ Disagree Why? ....

3. "The shifts of Fortune test the reliability of friends."
   —Cicero (106–43 B.C.E.), Roman statesman

   ☐ Agree ☐ Disagree Why? ....

4. "It is more shameful to distrust our friends than to be deceived by them."
   —Francois de La Rochefoucauld (1613–1680), French philosopher

   ☐ Agree ☐ Disagree Why? ....

5. "Animals are such agreeable friends; they ask no questions, they pass no criticisms."
   —George Eliot/Mary Ann Evans (1819–1880), English novel

   ☐ Agree ☐ Disagree Why? ....

6. "It is easier to forgive an enemy than to forgive a friend."
   —William Blake (1757–1827), English poet

   ☐ Agree ☐ Disagree Why? ....

7. "Have friends. It's a second existence."
   —Baltasar Gracian (1601–1658), Spanish philosopher

   ☐ Agree ☐ Disagree Why? ....

8. "Friendship is the finest balm for the pangs of despised love."
   — Jane Austen (1775 – 1817), English novelist

   ☐ Agree ☐ Disagree Why? ....

9. "Don't walk behind me, I may not lead. Don't walk in front of me, I may not follow. Just walk beside me and be my friend."
   —Albert Camus (1913–1960), French author/journalist, Nobel Prize winner (1957)

   ☐ Agree ☐ Disagree Why? ....

10. "A true friend is the most precious of possessions, and the one we take least thought about acquiring."
    —Francois de La Rochefoucauld (1613-1680), French philosopher

    ☐ Agree ☐ Disagree Why? ....

⭐ ON YOUR OWN

Write a letter, by hand or on a computer, to a friend that you have not communicated with recently. What have you been doing since you saw each other? Feel free to include photos, etc. You can share it with your group.

Chapter Notes

CHAPTER 11
PET PEEVES

SHARING COMPLAINTS

Sometimes things annoy us, and that's okay. Share your complaints and pet peeves with your partner. Discussing, sighing, and sharing can sometimes help us in difficult situations.

1. What annoys you? Do you have any pet peeves?

2. What are some things that you find impolite? Give examples.

3. How can salespeople be annoying? Can you give some examples?

4. Have you ever had serious email problems? How did you respond?

5. What technology bothers you? Why?

6. Do you quickly figure out how new appliances work?

7. What behavior do you often find offensive? Why?

8. What is litter? Have you seen any litterbugs? Where does litter bother you most?

9. What do you consider bad cell phone manners or habits?

10. When, or where, do you most often see people stressed?

11. What behavior might be considered irritating in a neighbor? Can you give an example of a difficult neighbor?

12. Is there a difference between assertive and aggressive?

13. How do aggressive people make you feel? How do you tend to respond?

14. Are there many aggressive drivers in your city? Is "road rage" a problem in Vietnam?

15. What behavior would be strange for a man, but normal for a woman?

16. What behavior might seem odd for a woman, but normal for a man?

17. Is there a double standard for men and women? How? Is this fair?

EXPANDING VOCABULARY

| annoy | bother | courtesy | impolite | litter |
| obnoxious | offended | pet | peeve | polite profanity |

annoy *verb*: to disturb or irritate.

• Loud traffic noises annoy me when I'm trying to sleep at night.

bother *verb*: to annoy, to disrupt or disturb; to make one feel bad

• Don't bother me while I'm talking on the phone.

"If you don't have anything nice to say, come sit by me."

—Alice Roosevelt Longworth (1884-1980), icon and Theodore Roosevelt's daughter

REMEMBER...

- Be clear.
- Be honest.
- Be fair.

ON YOUR OWN

Prepare a one-minute presentation on your biggest pet peeve that you may later give to the class.

....
....
....
....
....
....
....
....
....
....
....
....
....
....

courtesy *noun*: a kind or polite act; politeness.

- It's a common courtesy to hold a door open for others.

impolite *adjective*: poor behavior, rude

- It's impolite to spit on the floor.

litter *noun*: trash that can be seen on the street; garbage on the ground; *noun*: a number of dogs or cats born at the same time to the same mother.

- Litter has become a major problem in some large cities with trash all over the streets.
- My dog gave birth to a litter of six puppies.

obnoxious *adjective*: extremely annoying; bothersome.

- It's obnoxious to throw leftover food on the street and act like a litterbug.

offended *adjective*: feeling upset or insulted.

- I feel offended when you use ugly, vulgar, and rude words to insult me.

pet peeve *noun*: something which annoys or irritates a person;

- My biggest pet peeve is my neighbor's loud TV which keeps me awake.

polite *adjective*: good manners; respectful.

- Being polite just means thinking about someone else and their feelings.

profanity *noun*: a filthy word, offensive language.

- A parent should punish a child who uses profanity in public to insult neighbors.

ASKING QUESTIONS

A. Select five vocabulary words in this chapter, and write a question for each word. Remember to start your question with a question word (Who, What, Where, Why, How, Is, Do, When, etc.). You also want to end each question with a question mark (?). Underline each vocabulary word.

Example: Who is the most impolite person you know?

1...
2...
3...
4...
5...

B. Take turns asking and answering questions with your partner or group members.

PARAPHRASING PROVERBS

A. Read the following proverbs, and discuss them with your partner. What do they mean? Circle your favorites. Explain your choices.

- Recite "patience" three times and it will spare you a murder.—Korean

- This is done and I'm to blame. Therefore, know that I'm in shame.—Persian

- Control yourself: remember anger is only one letter short of danger. —American high school poster

- Love makes a good eye squint.—English

- The reputation of a thousand years may be determined by the conduct of one hour.—Japanese

- Hatred is as blind as love.

- If you empty a cup of wine in one gulp, you are a drunkard.

- So much to do, so little done.

B. Can you add two more?

- ....

- ....

THE CONVERSATION CONTINUES...

1. What table manners or eating styles make you frown or annoy you?

2. When, if ever, does snoring, sneezing, or coughing bother you?

3. Where do you find adults generally act their worst? Why?

4. How does a polite child act? How does a rude child behave?

5. Where do people learn good manners? What are good manners?

6. What do you dislike about living here?

7. Can you describe a polite boss? A very difficult boss?

8. How have co-workers or classmates annoyed you? What did they do? How did you handle the situation?

9. How have you handled working with rude customers? Are you able to keep your cool?

10. Does foul language, or profanity, upset you? When?

11. What obnoxious behavior have you had a strong negative reaction to?

12. Have you ever walked out of a movie? Were you offended? Why?

13. Are there personality traits that you find extremely disagreeable?

14. How can someone really make you "blow your lid" or explode? What brings out the worst in you? A family relative? A good friend?

15. What is something that once annoyed you that you have, over time, come to tolerate?

16. Have you seen any changes in what are considered good manners? What?

17. What is your advice for dealing with difficult, moody, or "toxic" people?

18. What are some social evils? Why?

19. Can you compare a pet peeve and a social evil?

20. How can people bring out your best side?

"Hatred is as blind as love."

—Irish proverb

Take turns reading these quotations out loud, and discuss them with your partner. Do you agree with the quotation? Disagree? Why? Mark your answer.

1. "The test of good manners is to be patient with bad ones."
   —Solomon ibn Gabriol (1021–1051), Hebrew poet/philosopher

   ☐ Agree ☐ Disagree Why? ....

2. "Good manners are made up of petty sacrifices."
   —Ralph Waldo Emerson (1803–1882), American essayist

   ☐ Agree ☐ Disagree Why? ....

3. "Be polite; write diplomatically; even in a declaration of war one observes the rules of politeness."
   —Otto von Bismarck (1815–1898), German aristocrat/statesman

   ☐ Agree ☐ Disagree Why? ....

4. "Never treat a guest like a member of the family—treat him with courtesy."
   —Evan Esar (1899–1935), American humorist

   ☐ Agree ☐ Disagree Why? ....

5. "Isn't it monstrous the way people go about saying things behind other people's backs that are absolutely and entirely true?"
   —Oscar Wilde (1854–1900), Irish author/playwright

   ☐ Agree ☐ Disagree Why? ....

6. "When you're down and out, something always turns up—usually the noses of your friends."
   —Orson Welles (1915–1985), American actor/director

   ☐ Agree ☐ Disagree Why? ....

7. "Those who do not complain are never pitied."
   —Jane Austen (1775-1819), English novelist

   ☐ Agree ☐ Disagree Why? ....

8. "There are bad manners everywhere, but an aristocracy is bad manners organized."
   —Henry James (1843-1916), American writer

   ☐ Agree ☐ Disagree Why? ....

9. "Kindness is the language which the deaf can hear and the blind can see."
   —Mark Twain (1835-1910), American writer

   ☐ Agree ☐ Disagree Why? ....

10. "I have the simplest taste. I am always satisfied with the best."
    —Oscar Wilde (1854-1900), Irish writer

    ☐ Agree ☐ Disagree Why? ....

Customer Complaints and Practicing Prepositions

We often need to use proper English to solve problems at work. Work with your conversation partner and find the right preposition to fill in the missing blank. Take turns reading sentences and determine which sentences are replies to complaints. The prepositions are grouped together for clarity. After filling in each group determine whether the speaker is making a complaint or responding to a complaint.

To

- I'm writing .... complain about your customer service helpline.
- I'm calling .... make a complaint.
- I wish .... make an inquiry about something on my monthly bill.
- I've been trying .... get through to you for two weeks.
- The order was delivered .... the wrong branch.
- I'm sorry that I didn't get back .... you sooner.
- The delay wasn't our fault. It was due .... the bad weather.

On

- The delivery arrived .... the wrong day.
- If you can't deliver .... time, we'll have to contact other suppliers.
- I would like to apologize .... behalf of Nippon Ham for any inconvenience.

For

- Please accept our apologies .... the inconvenience.
- We would like to offer you a discount on your next order to make up .... our mistake.
- Thank you .... bringing this matter to my attention.
- I'm sorry .... sending the documents to the wrong address.
- Who signed .... the delivery?

Of

- Please find a list .... the missing items.
- There were a number .... mistakes on the invoice.
- Several .... our delivery vehicles are out of service.
- We were closed for a number .... days due to the floods.

About

- I'm sorry. I'm calling to complain .... your payment system.
- I'm calling .... my order. It isn't here yet.
- I'd like to learn .... your refund policy.

Under

- The product is no longer .... warranty.
- We found your order .... someone else's name.
- Would you please look .... the counter to see if there are more?
- I'd like to see the shirt .... the blue one.

With

- I had some problems .... the instruction booklet.
- .... reference to your reminder of December 1, it seems to us that an error has been made.
- We are not satisfied .... the quality of the products.
- I have checked .... the staff involved, and they claim they were not responsible.

In

- .... fact, we had already paid the full bill the previous week.
- We will do our best to ensure that such mistakes do not occur again .... the future.
- Are you sure it was included .... the shipment?

Into

- We will look .... it right away and get back to you as soon as we can.
- I would be grateful if you could look .... the matter.

At

- I believe your sales department is .... fault.
- Would you please look _____ the bill I received?
- Our records show the package was received ____ your address.

By

- We strongly believe that the mistake was made .... your company.
- We will correct the mistake .... noon today.
- The part will be replaced .... the manufacturer.

EXERCISE
Write three consumer complaints with a preposition.

1...

2...

3...

Write three responses to consumer complaints with prepositions.

1...

2...

3...

Chapter Notes

....
....
....
....
....
....
....
....
....
....
....
....
....
....
....
....
....
....
....
....
....
....
....
....
....
....
....
....
....

CHAPTER 12
EXPLORING CITIES

SHARING URBAN STORIES

Cities can be confusing, exciting, and fast-paced. Some people love living in cities; and some people prefer living in the countryside. Share your experiences and feelings about cities with your partner.

1. Were you born in a city or the countryside? How far is your birthplace from here?

2. What do you like to do in cities? Why?

3. Which Vietnamese cities have you visited? How far is that from here?

4. How do people usually get around Vietnamese cities?

5. Can you tell me about a famous district in a Vietnamese city?

6. Have you been to Hanoi yet? How often?

7. What makes the capital of Vietnam an attractive city?

8. Can you describe some historic places in Hanoi?

9. Why do you think people love to go to Hoan Kiem Lake?

10. How has Hanoi changed over the last decade?

11. What adjectives describe Hanoi? Why?

12. Which other Vietnamese cities have important archaeological areas?

13. Which Vietnamese city do you know best? Why?

14. What do you like best about that city? Why?

15. Compare two Vietnamese cities. How are they similar? Different?

16. Why do you think people are attracted to Vietnam's growing cities?

EXPANDING VOCABULARY

| archaeology | attraction | beautify | capital | commute |
| hometown | landmark | skyscraper | slum | zoning |

archaeology *noun*: the study of historic sites and ancient buildings.

• Archaeology helped make Hue a World Heritage Site where archaeologists can study the city's many ancient buildings, beautiful temples, and royal palaces.

"Cities force growth, and make men talkative and entertaining, but they make them artificial."

—Ralph Waldo Emerson (1803-1882), American philosopher

attraction *noun*: a natural force which acts to bring people or things together.

• Halong Bay has become Vietnam's greatest tourist attraction.

beautify *verb*: to make beautiful.

• The government announced several projects to beautify the growing city.

capital *noun*: a city that is the seat of government in a country or state; *noun*: money invested and used to create more wealth.

• Hanoi is the charming capital of Vietnam.

• Adequate capital makes opening a new business much easier.

commute *noun*: the time or path of travel to your job from your home and back every day.

• My commute to campus is only 20 minutes by motorbike, but it used to take much longer when I rode my bicycle.

hometown *noun*: the city where a person was born.

• Danang is my hometown, but I have lived in Ho Chi Minh City for three years.

landmark *noun*: a place of historical or cultural importance; a significant event or idea.

• The Eiffel Tower in Paris, France and the Statue of Liberty in New York City are urban landmarks well-known around the world.

skyscraper *noun*: a high rise building in a city; a tall office tower.

• The tallest skyscraper in the world is in the Middle East, in Dubai.

slum *noun*: the poor, overcrowded section of a city.

• The fashionable neighborhood used to be a slum, but it has been rebuilt over time by new families and modern shops.

zoning *noun*: laws that restrict how property can be used in a specific area.

• The new zoning laws will beautify the crowded area and reduce traffic jams on the narrow streets.

ASKING QUESTIONS

A. Select five vocabulary words in this chapter, and write a question for each word. Remember to start your question with a question word (Who, What, When, Where, Why, How, Is, Are, Do, Does, etc). You also want to end each question with a question mark (?). Underline each vocabulary word.

Example: What are some local landmarks?

1...

2...

3...

4...

5...

B. Take turns asking and answering questions with your partner or group members.

✪ REMEMBER...

• Be alert.

• Be careful.

• Be humane.

★ ON YOUR OWN

List 10 cities from around the world. For each city, write down two words to describe that city. For example: Hue: beautiful, ancient.

1...
....
....
2...
....
....
3...
....
....
4...
....
....
5...
....
....
6...
....
....
7...
....
....
8...
....
....
9...
....
....
10 ....
....
....

PARAPHRASING PROVERBS

A. Read the following proverbs, and discuss them with your partner. What do they mean? Circle your favorites. Explain your choices.

- Rome wasn't built in a day.—Latin
- The city for wealth; the country for health.—English
- A city that sits on a hill can't be hid.—Greek
- A city is a place so big that no one counts.
- Go to the country to hear the news of town.—American

B. Can you add two more?

- ....
- ....

THE CONVERSATION CONTINUES...

1. What do you expect to find in a modern city? Why?
2. Have you traveled outside of Vietnam? Where did you go?
3. While traveling, were you ever afraid? Why?
4. While traveling, were you ever lost? Where were you?
5. Have you ever taken a tour? When?
6. Do you feel safer in cities or in rural areas? Why?
7. What is archaeology? How does archaeology help us understand cities?
8. Do you often go to museums in cities? Which would you like to see? Why?
9. Has any place surprised you? How was it different from what you expected?
10. Where would you like to travel next? Why? What would you most like to see?
11. Which cities have hosted the Olympics Games? Do you remember when?
12. Which cities have hosted World Cup championships?
13. Can you think of some famous urban landmarks?
14. Which world cities, outside of Vietnam, would you like to visit? Why?
15. In your opinion, what makes a city feel "civilized"? Why?

DISCUSSING QUOTATIONS

Take turns reading these quotations out loud, and discuss them with your partner. Do you agree with the quotation? Disagree? Why? Mark your answer.

1. "The people are the city."
   —William Shakespeare (1564-1616), English playwright

   ☐ Agree ☐ Disagree Why? ....

2. "It is men who make a city, not walls or ships."
   —Thucydides (460 BCE – 395 BCE), Greek historian

   ☐ Agree ☐ Disagree Why? ....

3. "City life: millions of people being lonesome (lonely) together."
   —Henry David Thoreau (1817-1862), American writer

   ☐ Agree ☐ Disagree Why? ....

4. "What you want is to have a city which everyone can admire as being something finer and more beautiful than he had ever dreamed of before."
   —James Bryce (1838-1922), American architect

   ☐ Agree ☐ Disagree Why? ....

5. "Paris is a city of…pleasures where four-fifths of the inhabitants die of grief."
   —Nicholas Chamfort (1741-1794), French writer

   ☐ Agree ☐ Disagree Why? ....

6. "Los Angeles is a city no worse than others; a city rich and vigorous and full of pride, a city lost and beaten and full of emptiness."
   —Raymond Chandler (1888-1959), American author of crime stories

   ☐ Agree ☐ Disagree Why? ....

7. "A city is a place where there is no need to wait for next week to get the answer to a question, to taste the food of any country, to find new voices to listen to and familiar ones to listen to again."
   —Margaret Mead (1901-1978), anthropologist

   ☐ Agree ☐ Disagree Why? ....

8. "I'd rather wake up in the middle of nowhere than in any city on earth."
   —Steve McQueen (1930-1980), American actor/movie star

   ☐ Agree ☐ Disagree Why? ....

9. "The city is a human zoo, not a concrete jungle."
   —Dr. Desmond Morris (1928- British zoologist

   ☐ Agree ☐ Disagree Why? ....

10. "The city must never be confused with the words that describe it. And yet, between one and the other, there is a connection."
    —Italo Calvino (1923-1985), Italian novelist

    ☐ Agree ☐ Disagree Why? ....

★ **EXPLORE A NEW CITY!**

Select one of the 10 cities that you would like to visit. Find out more about the city. Use the worksheet called "Be A Tourist". Be ready to talk about the city for a few minutes in a group next class. Your teacher may call for brave volunteers to present to the class.

Explore a New City!

Student Name .... Class ....

Teacher/School .... Date ....

Let's go explore a new city. Find an article—written in English—about a city that you want to visit. Carefully read the article, make a copy, and answer the questions below. Be prepared to share your research about an international city with your classmates.

1. Title:...

2. Author: .... 3. Length: ....

4. Publication: .... 5. Publication date: ....

6. What's the main idea? ....

....

....

7. How many sources were quoted? ....

8. Where there any illustrations? What kind? ....

....

....

9. What did you learn in this article? ....

....

....

10. What was the most interesting part for you? Why? ....

....

11. Write down 5 new vocabulary words, idioms, or expressions.

• ....

• ....

• ....

• ....

• ....

12. How would you rate the article on a scale from 1-10? Why? ....

13. Why did you choose this article? ....

www.CompellingConversations.com

Chapter Notes

....
....
....
....
....
....
....
....
....
....
....
....
....
....
....
....
....
....
....
....
....
....
....
....
....
....
....

CHAPTER 13
TALKING ABOUT MOVIES

CHATTING ABOUT FAVORITE FILMS

You can also start a conversation by asking for movie suggestions. Talk with your partner, and share your movie experiences.

1. Do you like movies? Where do you usually see movies?

2. How often do you watch movies? At home? In theatres?

3. Where do you find movies to watch at home?

4. Do you have cable television?

5. Do you own any movies? Which? Do you repeatedly watch them?

6. Have you figured out a way to see movies for free? How?

7. What might annoy you at a movie theatre? Using phones? Babies crying? Other?

8. Do you have a favorite movie theatre? A preferred place to sit?

9. Have you ever seen a celebrity or famous person? Where? Tell us about it.

10. Can you think of some tourist sights related to the movie industry?

11. Which Vietnamese movies do you like the most?

12. Which Vietnamese actors/actresses do you like the most? Why?

13. Have you ever seen movies being filmed? Where? What was the atmosphere?

14. Have you ever acted in a play or movie? Can you describe your experience?

VOCABULARY

With your partner, write definitions for five vocabulary words.

adapt	animation	blockbuster	cast	celebrity
director	famous	genre	popular	word of mouth

adapt *verb*: to change; modify.

- The English novel *Oliver Twist* has been adapted many times into many different films; some adaptations have been quite successful in depicting how poverty harms children.

animation *noun*: a moving cartoon, a technique used to make drawings come alive.

- *Finding Nemo* and *The Lion King* are two popular examples of animation.

"Talking about dreams is like talking about movies, since the cinema uses the language of dreams; years pass in a second and you can hop from one place to another."

—Federico Fellini (1920-1993), Italian film director

blockbuster *noun*: a very popular movie, often with expensive special effects; *adjective*: pertaining to a major success.

- The blockbuster *Avatar* made over $1 billion, used fantastic special effects, and inspired millions of movie fans.

cast *noun*: the actors in a play, show or movie; *verb*: to assign a role in a show.

- The *Harry Potter* series has a great cast of British actors and actresses.

celebrity *noun*: a famous person; a person who attracts media attention.

- After the movie *Titanic*, Kate Winslet became a celebrity.

director *noun*; the person who directs the actors and crew in the making of a film. They control a film's artistic and dramatic aspects.

- Stephen Spielberg is among the world's most famous directors.

famous *adjective*: well-known, recognized by most people.

- Hanoi is famous for its beauty.

genre *noun*: category of artistic endeavor having a particular form, content or technique.

- Romantic comedies are my favorite genre, but my boyfriend prefers action films.

popular *adjective*: well-liked, regarded with affection.

- *The Dark Knight* was a very popular film worldwide.

word of mouth *noun*: the spread of an idea or cultural event from person to person; an informal or personal information network.

- The film was not advertised, but became popular by word of mouth.

MOVIE GENRES

1. Which types (genres) of movies do you enjoy most? Why?

2. Can you think of an example of a good movie in five different categories?

3. Can you think of an example of a bad movie in three categories?

4. What makes your favorite films special or memorable?

5. Name a few movies that you disliked. Why did you dislike them?

6. Can you think of some books that have been adapted into movies? Did the adaptations work?

7. Did you have a favorite movie as a child? Teenager?

8. Did you have a favorite star as a child or teenager? Who? Why?

9. Do you know anybody who had a "crush" on a famous actor or actress?

10. Which movies have you seen more than once?

11. Do you have any favorite actors now? Why? How did they move you?

12. What actors, actresses, or directors would you like to have lunch with?

13. Do you have any favorite directors? Why? Which of that director's films influenced you?

⭐ **ON YOUR OWN**

Tell your classmates about your favorite movie. What makes it special? Who is in it? What's your favorite part? Why? Why do you recommend it? Keep your movie review short so everyone can share their favorite movies in class.

14. How do you decide which movie to see? Word of mouth? Ads? Awards? Reviews?

15. Which movies would you suggest a tourist to your country watch? Why?

16. What movies have you seen this year? Which do you recommend?

17. Do you think movies influence society or reflect society? How?

DISCUSSING QUOTATIONS

Take turns reading these quotations out loud, and discuss them with your partner. Do you agree with the quotation? Disagree? Why? Mark your answer.

1. "Movies are a fad. Audiences really want to see live actors on a stage."
   —Charlie Chaplin (1889–1977), British comedian and actor

   ☐ Agree ☐ Disagree Why? ....

2. "You know what your problem is? It's that you haven't seen enough movies—all of life's riddles are answered in the movies."
   —Steve Martin (1945–), American actor/comedian

   ☐ Agree ☐ Disagree Why? ....

3. "Watch this if you like, and if you don't, take a hike."
   —Clint Eastwood (1930–), actor, director, and producer

   ☐ Agree ☐ Disagree Why? ....

4. "It's the movies that have really been running things in America ever since they were invented. They show you what to do, how to do it, when to do it, how to feel about it, and how to look how you feel about it."
   —Andy Warhol (1928–1987), American artist

   ☐ Agree ☐ Disagree Why? ....

5. "We need families to start taking more responsibility in understanding which movie is good for their children and which movie is not."
   —Jet Li (1963–), Chinese actor and martial artist

   ☐ Agree ☐ Disagree Why? ....

6. "Movies are fun, but they're not a cure for cancer."
   —Warren Beatty (1937–), American actor, director, and producer

   ☐ Agree ☐ Disagree Why? ....

7. "I did a women's movie, and I'm not a woman. I did a gay movie, and I'm not gay. I learned as I went along."
   —Ang Lee (1954–), film director born in Taiwan

   ☐ Agree ☐ Disagree Why? ....

8. "My movies were the kind they show in prisons and airplanes because nobody can leave."
   —Burt Reynolds (1936–), American actor

   ☐ Agree ☐ Disagree Why? ....

⭐ MOVIE GENRES

- Action
- Adventure
- Animation
- Biography
- Children
- Comedy
- Crime/Detective
- Documentary
- Drama
- Epic
- Fantasy
- Foreign
- Historical
- Horror
- Melodrama
- Musical
- Mystery
- Romance
- Science Fiction
- Silent
- Suspense
- War

9. "Acting is not an important job in the scheme of things. Plumbing is."
   —Spencer Tracy (1900–1967), actor

   ☐ Agree ☐ Disagree Why?..

10. "Maybe every other American movie shouldn't be based on a comic book."
    —Bill Maher (1956–), American comedian

    ☐ Agree ☐ Disagree Why?..

11. "Life is like a movie, write your own ending. Keep believing, keep pretending."
    —Jim Henson (1936–1990), American creator of the Muppets

12. "The difference between life and the movies is that a script has to make sense, and life doesn't."
    —Joseph L. Mankiewicz (1909–1993), American screenwriter

    ☐ Agree ☐ Disagree Why?..

Be a Movie Critic!

Can you recommend a good movie? Select one of your favorite movies, go to www.imdb.com, and research the film. Use this worksheet to describe the movie, and prepare to share your favorite movie with your classmates.

1. Title .... 2. Genre ....

3. Date .... 4. Length .... 5. Director ....

6. Actors/Actresses ....

7. Awards? ....

8. How many times have you watched the movie? ....

PLOT INFORMATION:

9. Where does the movie take place? ....

....

10. When does the movie take place? ....

11. Who are the main characters? Can you briefly describe them? ....

....

....

12. What happens in the movie? ....

....

13. What makes the movie interesting? ....

....

14. What is the best part? Why? ....

....

15. Does the movie surprise the audience? How? ....

....

16. How did you feel when the movie ended? Why? ....

....

17. Is there anything else you want to tell me about your favorite movie? ....

....

18. Who do you think would also like this movie? Why? ....

....

19. On a scale on 1-5 stars, how do you rate this movie? ....

Chapter Notes

....

....

....

....

....

....

....

....

....

....

....

....

....

....

....

....

....

....

....

....

....

....

....

....

....

....

....

....

CHAPTER 14
LEARNING IN SCHOOL

SHARING SCHOOL STORIES

We have spent thousands of hours in schools, learned many skills, and collected many stories. Share your school stories with a classmate.

1. When did you first go to school? Was it an urban, a rural, or a suburban school?

2. How did you usually get to school? Did you walk, take a bus, or ride a bike or use another method?

3. How long was your commute to elementary school? High school?

4. How many students were usually in your class? What was the atmosphere like?

5. Do you remember the name of your elementary school? High school?

6. Did you attend a public or private school? Why?

7. Was there a school dress code? What were some other rules?

8. How would you describe your elementary school? Did you enjoy it?

9. Were your parents involved in your studies? How?

10. Were you given report cards? How often? What kind of grades did you get?

11. Can you describe the classroom conditions in your high school?

12. How large was your high school? What was the lunchroom like?

13. What subjects did you take in high school?

Did you choose your courses?

14. What was your favorite course? Why?

15. Were there any classes that you dreaded or hated? Why?

16. Did you have to take any exams?

Which exam was the most difficult? Why?

17. Was cheating common? Why? Did you ever cheat? How?

EXPANDING VOCABULARY

academic	adversity	bully	campus	dormitory
dress code	elementary	field trip	role model	tutor

"Education is an ornament in prosperity and a refuge in adversity."

—Aristotle (384-322), Greek philosopher

academic *adjective*: educational, related to school.

• Academic life offers many emotional and intellectual rewards to teachers, but relatively few financial ones since the pay is often low.

adversity *noun*: harsh conditions, suffering; bad luck or hardship.

• Adversity sometimes makes people, and nations, stronger as they learn to solve problems and overcome obstacles to reach independence.

bully *noun*: an aggressive person who threatens schoolmates; *verb* to scare or threaten a person.

• Bullies must be disciplined by school authorities.

• No nation can bully a strong Vietnam.

campus *noun*: school grounds.

• The campus is the center of academic life at many universities.

dress code *noun*: rules on what clothing is allowed in school.

• The school dress code prohibits short skirts and open-neck blouses.

elementary *adjective*: primary, basic; fundamental.

• Elementary school begins with kindergarten.

field trip *noun*: an organized trip a class takes away from campus.

• We took several field trips to both local and national museums.

report cards *noun*: the academic record of students.

• Look at my excellent report card!

role model *noun*: a person to admire or imitate; one who sets a good example.

• My father is a great role model.

tutor *noun*: a private teacher who helps a student outside of regular class.

• My TOEFL tutor gave me extra help with my English lessons after school.

ASKING QUESTIONS

A. Select five vocabulary words in this chapter, and write a question for each word. Remember to start your question with a question word (Who, What, When, Where, Why, How, Is, Are, Do, Does, etc.). You also want to end each question with a question mark (?). Underline each vocabulary word.

Example: Where is the school campus?

1...

2...

3...

4...

5...

B. Take turns asking and answering questions with your partner or group members.

REMEMBER...

• Study hard.

• Remain curious.

• Do your best.

What is the best class that you have had? Describe the teacher and the subject. Can you list three factors that made your favorite class special?

1...

2...

3...

PARAPHRASING PROVERBS

A. Read the following proverbs, and discuss them with your partner. What do they mean? Circle your favorites. Explain your choices.

- Study manners first, then learn to read and write.—Vietnamese
- Learning colors a man more than the deepest dye.—Chinese
- The dog near a school will learn to recite lessons in three years.—Korean
- He who is afraid to ask is ashamed of learning.—Danish
- We learn to walk by stumbling.—Bulgarian
- In time, even a bear can be taught to dance.—Yiddish
- Don't step on your teacher's shadow.—Korean

B. Can you add two more?

- ....
- ....

THE CONVERSATION CONTINUES...

1. Did you ever have a tutor, join a study group, or go to a cram school? Why?

2. Do you remember taking field trips? Where did you go?

3. How many years of formal education have you had?

4. Do you remember any bullying or violent fights at school? Were guns used?

5. Were you often given homework? Was it too much, too little, or just right?

6. What was your favorite place to study? Can you describe the area?

7. What after-school activities, clubs, or sports did you participate in?

8. What sports did the school compete in? Did they have a mascot?

9. What are you proud of achieving in your academic studies?

10. What was your best school year? Or what did you enjoy most about school?

11. What's your earliest school memory? Favorite memory?

12. Did you find a role model or mentor (teacher, coach) at your school? Who?

13. Have you kept in touch with anyone from your high school? Who? How?

14. Would you want your children to attend the schools that you attended? Why?

15. Can you compare and contrast schools in two countries?

16. Do you have any ideas on how to reform or improve schools?

DISCUSSING QUOTATIONS

Take turns reading these quotations out loud, and discuss them with your partner. Do you agree with the quotation? Disagree? Why? Mark your answer.

1. "It is impossible for a man to learn what he thinks he already knows."
   —Epictetus, (55-135), stoic philosopher

   ☐ Agree ☐ Disagree Why? ....

2. "Only the educated are free."
   —Epictetus (55-135), Stoic philosopher

   ☐ Agree ☐ Disagree Why? ....

3. "The wise are instructed by reason, average minds by experience, the stupid by necessity and the brute by instinct."
   —Marcus Cicero (106-43 BC) statesman

   ☐ Agree ☐ Disagree Why? ....

4. "Teach the tongue to say 'I don't know.'"
   —Maimonides (1135-1204), philosopher

   ☐ Agree ☐ Disagree Why? ....

5. "Nothing in life is to feared. It is only to be understood."
   —Marie Curie (1867-1934), Physicist

   ☐ Agree ☐ Disagree Why? ....

6. "Education is helping the child realize his potentialities."
   —Erich Fromm (1900-1980), Psychoanalyst

   ☐ Agree ☐ Disagree Why? ....

7. "They know enough who know how to learn."
   —Henry Adams (1838-1918), historian

   ☐ Agree ☐ Disagree Why? ....

8. "Education is a progressive discovery of our own ignorance."
   —Will Durant (1885-1981), historian

   ☐ Agree ☐ Disagree Why? ....

9. "The highest result of education is tolerance."
   —Helen Keller (1880-1968), author

   ☐ Agree ☐ Disagree Why? ....

10. "Education is a kind of continuing dialogue and a dialogue assumes, in the nature of the case, different points of view."
    —Robert Hutchins (1899-1977), educator

    ☐ Agree ☐ Disagree Why? ....

11. "Human history becomes more and more a race between education and catastrophe."
    —H.G. Wells (1866-1946), English novelist

    ☐ Agree ☐ Disagree Why? ....

12. "Perhaps the most valuable result of all education is the ability to make yourself do the thing you have to do, when it ought to be done, whether you like it or not."
    —Thomas H. Huxley (1825-1895) scientist

    ☐ Agree ☐ Disagree Why? ....

⭐ ON YOUR OWN

What are some effective ways to become an excellent student? Find advice on successful strategies to study—in English—on the Internet. Use the worksheet on the next page.

Collecting Academic Advice on the Internet

Student Name .... Class ....

Teacher/School .... Date .... :

Please find a video that provides tips for success in school or college— in English—that you would like to share with your classmates. The video might provide ways to improve test scores, get better grades, choosing a college, or some other aspect of academic success. Watch the video, take notes, and review the video for your classmates.

1. Video title: ....

2. Web address: .... 3. Length: ....

4. Creator: ....

5. Please describe the video: ....

....

....

....

6. What tips did the video provide? ....

....

....

7. Where do you think the video was produced? Why? ....

....

8. How practical did you find the advice? Why? ....

....

9. What was the strongest part? Why? ....

....

10. What was the weakest part? Why? ....

....

....

11. Who do you think is the audience for this video? ....

12. Why did you choose this video? ....

13. How would you rate this video on a 1-to-5 scale? Why? ....

....

chapter Notes

_____

_____

_____

_____

_____

_____

_____

_____

_____

_____

_____

_____

_____

_____

_____

_____

_____

_____

_____

_____

_____

_____

_____

_____

_____

_____

_____

CHAPTER 15

What Do You Think?

BRIDGING DIFFERENCES

Harmony is often important, but sometimes we still find ourselves disagreeing with loved ones, close friends, and co-workers. Therefore, we have to find ways to resolve the conflict in a respectful way. Sometimes we just listen and postpone an awkward discussion. Sometimes we try to find agreement and focus on where we agree. And sometimes we need to identify and express our disagreement so we can solve problems together.

The following phrases let you state your position clearly while keeping the conversation friendly. Read all phrases aloud.

Expressing agreement	Expressing disagreement
That's right.	Sorry, I disagree.
Absolutely.	I partially agree.
That's true.	That doesn't seem completely true.
I believe that	Sorry, I don't share that belief.
That's a good idea.	While that sounds good, it may not work.
This explains A, B, and C.	What about X, Y, or Z?
That's right on point.	That seems a bit off point.
I concur	Sorry, I can't completely agree.
I agree	I don't agree.
That's valid.	That's invalid.
I accept that.	I reject that.
I support that.	I don't support that idea.
That's a good idea!	Here's a better idea!
I definitely agree	I'm not sure I agree.
You should agree with me.	We agree on some points.
That sounds logical.	Is that really logical?
It's simple	Or is it complicated?

EXPANDING VOCABULARY

accept	acceptance	agreement	disagreement	assume
assumption	concur	consequences	solve	solution

Accept *verb*: to say yes, to agree, to concur.

• Thuy accepted the invitation to dinner.

Acceptance *noun:* the act of agreeing, the act of receiving something offered.

Her acceptance of his marriage proposal made everyone smile.

Agreement *noun:* the act of agreeing, a contract.

• The agreement was fair so we signed it.

Disagreement *noun:* the act of disagreeing, having different ideas and emotions.

• The disagreement seems silly now, but we were very upset at the time.

Assume *verb:* to accept without evidence, to believe without question.

• Let's assume that all parents love children, and always want the best for them.

Assumption *noun:* the act of taking something for granted, an unquestioned idea.

• The assumption that "newer means better" can sometimes be wrong.

Concur *verb:* to agree with, to support.

Hong concurred with his co-workers that they were lucky to have good jobs.

Consequences *noun:* the result or outcome of something.

Thich's decision to move to Hanoi had many consequences.

Solve *verb:* to find the answer, to work something out.

• Engineers solve problems by examining facts, considering alternatives, and making calculations.

Solution *noun:* the act of solving problems, finding answers.

• The simplest solution is sometimes the best solution, but sometimes the simplest solution doesn't really solve the problem.

ASKING QUESTIONS

A. Select five vocabulary words in this chapter, and write a question for each word. Remember to start your question with a question word (Who, What, Where, When, Why, How, Is, Are, Do, Did, Does, etc). You also want to end each question with a question mark (?). Underline each vocabulary word.

Example: Is that <u>assumption</u> reasonable?

1...

2...

3...

4...

5. ....

B. Take turns asking and answering questions with your partner or group members.

> **"Nobody minds having what is too good for them."**
>
> —Jane Austen (1775-1821), English novelist

DISCUSSING PROVERBS

Do you agree or disagree with the following proverbs? Why? Discuss with your partner.

1. The best things in life are free.
☐ Agree ☐ Disagree Why? ....

2. Children should be seen and not heard.
☐ Agree ☐ Disagree Why? ....

3. Spare the rod and spoil the child.
☐ Agree ☐ Disagree Why? ....

4. Money is the root of all evil.
☐ Agree ☐ Disagree Why? ....

5. Honesty is the best policy.
☐ Agree ☐ Disagree Why? ....

6. It's better to have loved and lost than never to have loved at all.
☐ Agree ☐ Disagree Why? ....

7. Behind every successful man there's a woman.
☐ Agree ☐ Disagree Why? ....

8. The end justifies the means.
☐ Agree ☐ Disagree Why? ....

9. Winning is everything.
☐ Agree ☐ Disagree Why? ....

10. Better to be a live dog than a dead lion.
☐ Agree ☐ Disagree Why? ....

11. Persistence pays.
☐ Agree ☐ Disagree Why? ....

12. There is no good war and no bad peace.
☐ Agree ☐ Disagree Why? ....

13. Your best friend is yourself.
☐ Agree ☐ Disagree Why? ....

14. Never judge a movie by its preview.
☐ Agree ☐ Disagree Why? ....

15. You can't keep a good man down.
☐ Agree ☐ Disagree Why? ....

16. A closed mouth catches no flies.
☐ Agree ☐ Disagree Why? ....

17. The best defense is a good offense.
☐ Agree ☐ Disagree Why? ....

18. Money makes the world go round.
☐ Agree ☐ Disagree Why? ....

www.CompellingConversations.com

MAKE NOTES AND ASK QUESTIONS

Choose a proverb from the previous section about which you and your conversation partner disagree. Spend five minutes thinking of situations to support your point of view. Then discuss your opinions in a friendly, respectful way. Use some of the phrases at the beginning of this chapter to keep the conversation flowing. Write down the proverb that you will discuss.

SEEKING CLARIFICATION

Sometimes we need more information to better understand each other, and reach an agreement. Read each of these phrases aloud to your partner.

- Can you clarify that?
- Can you explain your ideas more?
- So?
- What do you mean?
- Can you rephrase that?
- Why do you say that?
- Can you give another example?
- Have you considered?
- What if the situation were a bit different?
- What if?
- How far would you go?
- Are you sure? Why are you so sure?
- What's your source for that bit of information?
- How do you know?
- Can you imagine some alternatives?
- Is there another possibility?

DISCUSSING PROVERBS PART II

Consider each of the following common statements, attitudes, or proverbs. Which statement of agreement or disagreement best expresses your reaction?

1. Seeing is believing.
2. Appearances are deceiving.
3. Beauty promises happiness.
4. Be good and you will be happy.
5. No pain, no gain.
6. No pain, no pain.
7. The bigger, the better.
8. Less is more.
9. The unexpected always happens.
10. The sun rises every morning.

⭐ ON YOUR OWN

Learning to politely discuss and solve problems is a vital workplace skill. We should, for instance, always carefully listen to make sure we understand a problem before we express our opinion. Write five other guidelines that people can follow to have productive, positive conversations when they disagree about something. Be prepared to explain your answers.

1...

2...

3...

4...

5...

- Make notes.
- Ask questions.
- Find solutions.

11. You get what you pay for.

12. A penny saved is a penny earned.

13. Two can live as cheaply as one.

14. Bad news travels fast.

15. Liars should have good memories.

16. Life is not a popularity contest.

17. Counting your money is how you keep score.

18. You can't take it with you.

19. Time heals all wounds.

20. Never forget; never forgive.

21. Don't throw your pearls before swine.

22. A donkey prefers hay to gold.

23. Honesty is the best policy.

24. The early bird catches the worm.

25. Two heads are better than one.

ASKING QUESTIONS WITH PROVERBS

We've studied proverbs throughout this book. Ask five questions using a proverb.

Example: Do you agree that time heals all wounds?

1...

2...

3...

4...

5...

DISCUSSING QUOTATIONS

Take turns reading these quotations out loud, and discuss them with your partner. Do you agree with the quotation? Disagree? Why? Mark your answer.

1. "True love is like ghosts, which everybody talks about and few have seen."
   —Francois Duc De La Rochefoucauld (1613-1680), French writer
   ☐ Agree ☐ Disagree Why? ....

2. "Do not anticipate trouble or worry about what may never happen. Keep in the sunlight."
   —Benjamin Franklin (1705-1790), American statesman/scientist
   ☐ Agree ☐ Disagree Why? ....

3. "Nobody minds having what is too good for them."
   —Jane Austen (1775-1821), English novelist
   ☐ Agree ☐ Disagree Why? ....

4. "Nothing is so dangerous as an ignorant friend; a wise enemy is much better."
   —Jean de La Fontaine (1621-1695), French poet
   ☐ Agree ☐ Disagree Why? ....

5. "It is only with the heart that one can see rightly; what is essential is invisible to the eye."
   — Antoine de Saint-Exupery (1900 – 1944), French writer and pilot
   ☐ Agree ☐ Disagree Why? ....

6. "It was the best of times; it was the worst of times."
   —Charles Dickens (1812-1870), English novelist
   ☐ Agree ☐ Disagree Why? ....

7. "If two ride on a horse, one must ride behind."
   —William Shakespeare (1564-1616), great English playwright
   ☐ Agree ☐ Disagree Why? ....

8. "Experience is the name everyone gives their mistakes."
   —Oscar Wilde (1854-1900), Irish playwright
   ☐ Agree ☐ Disagree Why? ....

9. "Always do the right thing. This will gratify some and astonish the rest."
   —Mark Twain (1835-1910), American writer
   ☐ Agree ☐ Disagree Why? ....

10. "A problem is a chance for you to do your best."
    —Duke Ellington (1890-1974), Jazz composer and band leader
    ☐ Agree ☐ Disagree Why? ....

"In the middle of a difficulty lies opportunity."

—Albert Einstein (1879 -1955), Time Magazine Man of the 20th Century

Problem-Solution Worksheet

The English proverb "two heads are better than one" is often true. Solving problems can often be difficult. Working with your partner, focus on a problem—at school, at work, or in the local city—and find a reasonable solution together. Please follow this classic problem-solution method widely used in engineering and the sciences to solve problems. Be ready to share your process and conclusions in a short presentation next class.

DEFINE THE PROBLEM

Background ....

Problem ....

Short-term effects ....

Long-term effects...

FIND THE BEST SOLUTION

Possible solution ....

• Advantage..

• Disadvantage ....

Possible solution ....

• Advantage..

• Disadvantage ....

Possible solution ....

• Advantage..

• Disadvantage ....

Possible solution ....

• Advantage..

• Disadvantage ....

Best Solution ....

Reasons:

1. ....

2. ....

3. ....

www.CompellingConversations.com

Chapter Notes

_____

_____

_____

_____

_____

_____

_____

_____

_____

_____

_____

_____

_____

_____

_____

_____

_____

_____

_____

_____

_____

_____

_____

_____

_____

_____

_____

Appendix

"All's well that ends well."

—William Shakespeare
(1564–1616), playwright and poet

To English Students and Teachers

We want you to speak as much English as possible, both in and outside of your English classes. These extra materials can be used to deepen the classroom experience, for homework, or for self-study. These bonus materials are optional and supplemental—but clearly recommended.

Time restrictions and class sizes often limit the use of these supplemental activities. Many chapters include opportunities for students to give brief presentations. Feedback is helpful so we can learn what our audience heard and thought. Therefore, we have included forms for both instructor and peer feedback. Although peer evaluation is seldom used in many Vietnamese classrooms, peer feedback forms provide valuable information. It's also considered a recommended "best practice" internationally because the entire audience can ask questions and share ideas.

The next two worksheets, Reviewing Pronunciation Tips and Collecting Job Interview advice, can be used in both English classes and on your own. The Reviewing Pronunciation Tips can also be used over and over. Many adult and university students, of course, want to prepare for future job interviews. The internet provides many exceptional videos that provide insights into this often stressful process. Practice, as the proverb goes, makes perfect.

The Academic Word list is highly recommended if you plan to go to college or take the TOEFL or IELTS exams. The vocabulary will also help prepare students who want to work for international business companies or plan to take the TOEIC exam.

Finally, speaking with native English speakers can be both exciting and difficult. We hope that you choose to speak English more outside of the English classroom "in the real world." Sometimes planning a conversation in advance makes it easier. The six surveys here provide a "map" for short, comfortable English conversations with international tourists or workers in Vietnam. The surveys are arranged from simplest to the most difficult. Some English teachers will assign these surveys as homework or test, but they can also be used for self-study.

We want to share these bonus worksheets so you can continually improve your English and create your own compelling conversations both inside and outside the classroom.

- Student Presentation: Instructor Evaluation

- Student Presentation: Peer Response and a Question

- Reviewing Pronunciation Tips on the Internet

- The Academic Word List

- Surveys 1-6 for Speaking to International Visitors and Workers.

Student Presentation: Instructor Evaluation

1. Speaker: ....

2. Topic: ....

3. Date: .... 4. Time: ....

5. What was good to see in their presentation? ....

....

....

....

....

6. What could have been better? What still needs to be improved? ....

....

....

....

....

7. Other observations and tips: ....

....

....

....

....

8. Two tips for the student to improve their English speaking skills:

- ....

....

....

- ....

....

....

Student Presentation: Peer Response and a Question

Please provide feedback to your classmates on their presentations.

1. Speaker: ....

2. Topic: ....3. Date: ....

4. What was good to see in this presentation? ....

....

....

....

....

....

....

....

5. What could have been better? What still needs to be improved? ....

....

....

....

....

....

....

6. Other observations and tips: ....

....

....

....

....

....

....

7. Please write a question to ask the speaker about the topic. ....

....

Reviewing Pronunciation Tips on the Internet

Student Name .... Class ....

Teacher/School .... Date .... :

Please find a video on the Internet that reviews English pronunciation that you would like to share with your class-mates. Watch the video, take notes, and review it for your classmates.

1. Video title: ....

2. Web address: ....3. Length: ....

4. Creator: ....

5. Please describe the video: ....

....

....

6. What pronunciation tips did the video provide?..

....

....

7. Which words or sounds did the video focus on?..

....

....

8. How practical did you find the advice? Why? ....

....

9. What was the strongest part? Why?..

....

....

10. What was the weakest part? Why? ....

....

....

11. Who do think is the target audience for this video? ....

12. Why did you choose this video? ....

....

13. How would you rate this video on a 1-to-5 scale? Why?...

The Academic Word List

What is the Academic Word List? Why does it matter? How can it help you get a higher TOEFL Score?

Let's start with what many Vietnamese students hoping to go to college or study abroad already know. TOEFL scores count and focusing on the Academic Word List (AWL) helps students score higher on the TOEFL—across the curriculum.

English teachers naturally notice and appreciate a strong vocabulary, and academic writing requires a more formal register than casual oral speech. Standardized tests also reward a rich vocabulary and often explicitly test vocabulary skills. Nuance and precision can also be displayed by finding the appropriate word. Therefore, English language learners naturally seek to develop a strong academic vocabulary in order to succeed as college and university students.

Yet what are the key words that a college student needs for academic success in English? Professor Averil Coxhead at the School of Linguistics and Applied Language Studies at Victoria University of Wellington, New Zealand studied a wide range of academic texts across disciplines in the late 1990s. He culled 570 word families that he deemed vital for college preparation and created the Academic Word List. The list was further divided into 10 sub-lists, from the most frequent to the least frequent. (We've alphabetized the 10 sub-sets to easily look up words in the dictionary.)

Because of Coxhead's systematic approach and the clear need for this type of focused vocabulary list to help ambitious, college bound international students, the AWL quickly established itself within academic high schools around the world. Many intensive English programs also adopted the AWL for their college prep programs, creating a niche within the ESL/EFL world. Although an intense controversy has arisen over the extensive focus on this vocabulary list, motivated students (like you!) should become at least familiar with the AWL.

Let's begin with better English conversations in our English classrooms. Adding more AWL words and teaching explicit vocabulary enrichment exercises—in your writing and speaking—is a simple, effective method. Please pay extra attention to these words in your academic courses.

Here for your reading pleasure is the entire Academic Word List (AWL) in 10 subsections.

SUBLIST 1

analysis
approach
area
assessment
assume
authority
available
benefit
concept
consistent
constitutional
context
contract
create
data
definition
derived
distribution
economic
environment
established
estimate
evidence
expert
factors
financial
formula
function
identified
income
indicate
individual
interpretation

involved
issues
labour
legal
legislation
major
method
occur
percent
period
policy
principle
procedure
process
required
research
response
role
section
sector
significant
similar
source
specific
structure
theory
variables

SUBLIST 2

achieve
acquisition
administration
affect
appropriate

aspects
assistance
categories
chapter
commission
community
complex
computer
conclusion
conduct
construction
consequences
consumer
credit
cultural
design
distinction
elements
equation
evaluation
features
final
focus
impact
injury
institute
investment
items
journal
maintenance
normal
obtained
participation
perceived

positive
potential
previous
primary
purchase
range
region
regulations
relevant
resident
resources
restricted
security
select
site
sought
strategies
survey
text
tradition
transfer

SUBLIST 3

alternative
circumstance
comments
compensation
component
consent
considerable
constant
constraints
contribution
convention

coordination
core
corporate
corresponding
criteria
deduction
demonstrate
dominant
document
emphasis
ensure
excluded
framework
funds
illustrated
immigration
implies
initial
instance
interaction
justification
layer
link
location
maximum
minorities
negative
outcomes
partnership
philosophy
physical
proportion
published
reaction

registered
reliance
removed
scheme
sequence
sex
shift
specified
sufficient
task
technical
techniques
technology
validity
volume

SUBLIST 4
access
adequate
annual
apparent
approximate
attitudes
attributed
civil
code
communication
commitment
concentration
conference
contrast
cycle
debate
despite

dimensions
domestic
emerged
error
ethnic
goals
granted
hence
hypothesis
implementation
implications
imposed
integration
internal
investigation
job
label
mechanism
obvious
occupational
option
output
overall
parallel
parameters
phase
predicted
principal
prior
professional
project
promote
regime
resolution

retained
series
statistics
status
stress
subsequent
sum
summary
undertaken

SUBLIST 5
academic
adjustment
alter
amendment
aware
capacity
challenge
clause
compounds
conflict
consultation
contact
decline
draft
discretion
equivalent
enable
energy
enforcement
entities
evolution
expansion
exposure

external
facilitate
fundamental
generated
generation
image
liberal
license
logic
marginal
medical
mental
modified
monitoring
network
notion
objective
orientation
perspective
precise
prime
psychology
pursue
ratio
rejected
revenue
stability
styles
substitute
sustainable
symbolic
target
transition
trend

version
welfare
whereas
monitoring

SUBLIST 6
abstract
accurate
acknowledged
aggregate
allocation
assigned
attached
author
bond
brief
capable
cited
cooperative
discrimination
display
diversity
domain
edition
enhanced
estate
exceed
expert
explicit
federal
fees
flexibility
furthermore
gender

ignored
incentive
incidence
incorporated
index
inhibition
initiatives
input
instructions
intelligence
interval
lecture
migration
minimum
ministry
motivation
neutral
nevertheless
overseas
preceding
presumption
rational
recovery
revealed
scope
subsidiary
tapes
trace
transformation
transport
underlying
utility

SUBLIST 7

adaptation
adults
advocate
aid
channel
chemical
classical
comprehensive
comprise
confirmed
converted
contrary
couple
decades
definite
deny
differentiation
disposal
dynamic
eliminate
empirical
equipment
extract
file
finite
foundation
global
grade
guarantee
hierarchical
identical
ideology
inferred

innovation
insert
intervention
isolated
media
mode
paradigm
phenomenon
priority
prohibited
publication
quotation
release
reverse
simulation
solely
somewhat
submitted
successive
survive
thesis
topic
transmission
ultimately
unique
visible
voluntary

SUBLIST 8

abandon
accompany
accumulation
ambiguous
appendix

appreciation
arbitrary
automatically
bias
chart
clarity
commodity
complement
conformity
contemporary
contradiction
crucial
currency
denote
detected
deviation
displacement
dramatic
eventually
exhibit
exploitation
fluctuations
guidelines
highlighted
implicit
induced
inevitably
infrastructure
inspection
intensity
manipulation
minimizes
nuclear
offset

paragraph
plus
practitioners
predominantly
prospect
radical
random
reinforced
restore
revision
schedule
tension
termination
theme
thereby
uniform
vehicle
via
virtually
visual
widespread

SUBLIST 9

accommodation
analogous
anticipated
assurance
attained
bulk
behalf
ceases
coherence
coincide
commenced

concurrent	refine	integrity
confined	relaxed	intrinsic
controversy	restraints	invoked
conversely	revolution	levy
concurrent	rigid	likewise
device	route	nonetheless
devoted	scenario	notwithstanding
diminished	sphere	odd
distorted	subordinate	ongoing
duration	supplementary	panel
ethical	suspended	persistent
erosion	team	posed
format	temporary	reluctant
founded	trigger	so-called
incompatible	unified	straightforward
inherent	vision	undergo
insights	violation	whereby
integral		
intermediate		
manual	**SUBLIST 10**	
mature	adjacent	
mediation	albeit	
military	assembly	
minimal	collapse	
mutual	colleagues	
norms	compiled	
overlap	conceived	
passive	convinced	
portion	depression	
preliminary	encountered	
protocol	enormous	
qualitative	forthcoming	
	inclination	

Source: Wikitionary – Academic Word List accessed on 2/15/09 and alphabetized on 6/22/10.

Survey #1: Interviewing International Visitors

Many visitors will be glad to speak with you if they know that you just want to practice your English.

Your name: ....

Location: ....Date: ....

1. Can I ask you a few questions for my English class?

Person interviewed: ....

2. Where are you from? ☐ Europe ☐ North America ☐ Asia ☐ Other

3. What brings you to Vietnam? ☐ Tourism ☐ Business ☐ Both

4. How long have you been in Vietnam? ☐ 5 days or less ☐ 6-13 days ☐ 2 weeks- 2 months ☐ Longer ....

5. What do you like about Vietnam? ☐ Food ☐ People ☐ Shopping ☐ Museums ☐ Sights ☐ Other

....

....

6. What else do you hope to see or do in Vietnam before you leave?

....

....

7. Will you be taking souvenirs from Vietnam back with you? What kind? Why? ....

....

....

....

8. How can you describe your visit? ....

....

....

....

9. Will you recommend a visit to Vietnam to your family and friends? ☐ Absolutely ☐ Probably ☐ Maybe ☐ No

10. Would you please rate my English based on our conversation?

☐ Excellent ☐ Very good ☐ Good ☐ Okay ☐ Needs improvement

Thank you for your time and talking with me today.

Survey #2: Interviewing International Visitors

Many visitors will be glad to speak with you if they know that you just want to practice your English.

Your name...

Location: ....Date:..

1. Can I ask you a few short questions for my English class?

Person interviewed:...

2. Where are you from? ....

3. Why did you come to Vietnam? ....

4. How did you prepare for your visit here? ....

....

5. How long have you been in Vietnam?...

6. What do you like about visiting Vietnam?..

....

7. Which Vietnamese dishes have you tried?..

....

8. How does the food here compare with the food in your country?....................................

....

9. Can you compare shopping here with your country?..

....

10. How would you describe your visit so far?..

....

11. Can you share three tips for other visitors coming to Vietnam? ....

....

12. Finally, what will you tell your friends and relatives about your visit here? ....

....

BONUS: Would you please rate my English based on our conversation?

☐ Excellent ☐ Very good ☐ Good ☐ Okay ☐ Needs improvement

Thank you for your time and talking with me today.

Survey #3: Interviewing International Visitors

Many visitors will be glad to speak with you if they know that you just want to practice your English.

Your name:...

Location: ....Date:.......................................

1. Can I ask you a few short questions for my English class?

Person interviewed:...

2. Where are you from? ....

3. Why did you come to Vietnam? ....

4. How much time have you spent in Vietnam so far? ....

5. What do you like most about being in Vietnam? ....

....

6. Okay, what have you seen so far in ....?

7. How do you travel from one place to another? Do you walk? Ride a motorcycle? ....

8. How about longer distances? ....

9. Are you planning to go to Hanoi? ....

10. Will you be going to Halong Bay? ....

11. And do you expect to go to Hue and Central Vietnam?..

12.What are some other places you would like to see in Vietnam? Why? ....

....

13.What's your best memory of Vietnam so far? Why?...

....

....

14. How would you describe your trip so far? Why? ....

....

....

15. Will you recommend a visit to Vietnam to your family and friends? ....

BONUS: Would you please rate my English based on our conversation?

☐Excellent ☐Very good ☐Good ☐Okay ☐Needs improvement

Survey #4: Interviewing International Visitors

Many visitors will be glad to speak with you if they know that you just want to practice your English.

Your name:...

Person interviewed:..

Location: ....Date: ....

1. Can I ask you a few short questions for my English class?

2. Where are you from? ....

3. Why did you come to Vietnam? ....

4. How much time have you spent in Vietnam so far? ....

5. What do you like most about being in Vietnam? ....

....

6. Okay, what have you seen so far in ....?

7. How do go from one place to another? Do you walk? Ride a motorcycle? ....

8. How about longer distances? ....

9. Are you planning on to Hanoi? ....

10. Will you be going to Halong Bay? ....

11. And do you expect to go to Hue and Central Vietnam? ....

12. What are some other places you would like to see in Vietnam? Why? ....

....

....

13. What's your best memory of Vietnam so far? Why? ....

....

14. How would you describe your trip so far? Why? ....

....

....

15. So, will you be recommending visiting Vietnam to your family and friends? ....

Would you please rate my English based on our conversation today?

☐ Excellent ☐ Very good ☐ Good ☐ Okay ☐ Needs improvement

Survey #5: Interviewing International Visitors

Many visitors will be glad to speak with you if they know that you just want to practice your English.

Your name:..

Location: ....Date: ....

1. Can I ask you a few short questions for my English class?

Person interviewed:..

2. Where are you from? ....

3. Why did you come to...?

4. How much time have you spent in..?

5. What do you like most about being in ....?

6. Okay, what have you seen so far in ....?

7. What traditional dishes have you tried? ....

8. Have you found any bargains shopping yet? What? ....

9. How do you travel from one place to another? Do you walk? Take a bus? Other? ....

10. Are you planning to travel to another city? ....

11. Will you be going to ....?

12. And do you expect to go to ....?

13. What are some other places you would like to see?..

Why?...

14. What's your best memory of ....?

Why?...

15. How would you describe your trip?...

Why?...

....

16. So, will you recommend visiting...to your family and friends?

Would you please rate my English based on our conversation today?

☐ Excellent ☐ Very good ☐ Good ☐ Okay ☐ Needs improvement

Survey #6: Interviewing International Visitors

Many visitors will be glad to speak with you if they know that you just want to practice your English.

Your name:..

Location: ....Date: ....

1. What's your name? ....

2. Where are you from? ....

3. What brings you to Vietnam? ....

4. Can you share your first impressions? ....

5. What beautiful sights have you seen? ....

6. What Vietnamese food have you tried? ....

Do you have a favorite dish? ....

7. What activities or places have you enjoyed the most? Why? ....

....

....

8. What else do you hope to see or do in Vietnam before you leave? ....

....

9. Will you be taking souvenirs from Vietnam back with you? What kind? Why? ....

....

10. Can you choose five adjectives to describe your visit here? ....

....

....

BONUS

11. .... ?

12. .... ?

Thank you for your time and talking with me today.

Bibliography

21st Century Dictionary of Quotations. Dell Publishing, 1993.

Ackerman, Mary Alice. *Conversations on the Go.* Search Institute, 2004.

Akbar, Fatollah. *The Eye of an Ant: Persian Proverbs and Poems.* Iranbooks, 1995.

Ben Shea, Noah. *Great Jewish Quotes: Five Thousand Years of Truth and Humor from the Bible to George Burns.* Ballantine Books, 1993.

Berman, Louis A. *Proverb Wit and Wisdom: A Treasury of Proverbs, Parodies, Quips, Quotes, Cliches, Catchwords, Epigrams, and Aphorisms.* Perigee Book, 1997.

Bierce, Ambrose. *The Devil's Dictionary.* Dover Publications, 1993.

Bullivant, Alison. *The Little Book of Humorous Quotations.* Barnes & Noble Books, 2002.

Byrne, Robert. *1,911 Best Things Anybody Ever Said.* Ballantine Books, 1988.

Cohen, M. J. *The Penguin Dictionary of Epigrams.* Penguin, 2001.

Esar, Evan. *20,000 Quips and Quotes.* Barnes & Noble Books. 1995.

Frank, Leonard Roy. *Freedom: Quotes and Passages from the World's Greatest Freethinkers.* Random House, 2003.

Galef, David. *Even Monkeys Fall From Trees: The Wit and Wisdom of Japanese Proverbs.* Tuttle Publishing, 1987.

Galef, David. *Even a Stone Buddha Can Talk: More Wit and Wisdom of Japanese Proverbs.* Tuttle Publishing, 2000.

Gross, David C. and Gross, Esther R.. *Jewish Wisdom: A Treasury of Proverbs, Maxims, Aphorisms, Wise Sayings, and Memorable Quotations.* Walker and Company, 1992.

Gross, John. *The Oxford Book of Aphorisms.* Oxford University Press, 1987.

Habibian, Simin K. *1001 Persian-English Proverbs: Learning Language and Culture Through Commonly Used Sayings.* Third Edition. Ibex Publishers, 2002.

Jacobs, Ben and Hjalmarsson, Helena. *The Quotable Book Lover.* Barnes & Noble, 2002.

Jarski, Rosemarie. *Wisecracks: Great Lines from the Classic Hollywood Era.* Contemporary Books, 1999.

Lewis, Edward and Myers, Robert. *A Treasury of Mark Twain: The Greatest Humor of the Greatest American Humorist.* Hallmark Cards, 1967.

McLellan, Vern. *Quips, Quotes, and Quests.* Harvest Books, 1982.

MacHale, Des. *Wit.* Andrews McMeel Publishing, 2003.

McWilliams, Peter. *Life 101: Everything We Wish We Had Learned About Life In School—But Didn't.* Prelude Press, 1991.

The Oxford Dictionary of Quotations, 5th Edition. Oxford University Press, 1999.

Peter, Dr. Laurence J. *Peter's Quotations: Ideas for Our Time.* William Morrow, 1977.

Pickney, Maggie. *Pocket Positives For Our Times.* The Five Mile Press, 2002.

Pickney, Maggie. *The Devil's Collection: A Cynic's Dictionary.* The Five Mile Press, 2003.

Platt, Suzy. *Respectfully Quoted: A Dictionary of Quotations.* Barnes & Noble Books, 1993.

Poole, Garry. *The Complete Book of Questions.* Willow-Creek Association, 2003.

Rado, Adam. *Conversation Pieces.* Aethron Press. 2001.

Reader's Digest Quotable Quotes: Wit and Wisdom for All Occasions From America's Most Popular Magazine. Reader's Digest, 1997

Rosten, Leo. *Rome Wasn't Burned in a Day; The Mischief of Language.* Doubleday, 1972.

Rosten, Leo. *Leo Rosten's Carnival of Wit.* Penguin Books USA, 1994.

Shalit, Gene. *Great Hollywood Wit: A Glorious Cavalcade of Hollywood Wisecracks, Zingers, Japes, Quips, Slings, Jests, Snappers, and Sass from the Stars.* St. Martin's Griffin, 2002

Simpson, James Beasley. *Best Quotes of '54, '55, '56.* Thomas Y. Crowell Company, 1957.

Stavropoulos, Steven. *The Wisdom of the Ancient Greeks: Timeless Advice on the Senses, Society, and the Soul.* Barnes & Noble Books, 2003.

Sullivan, George. *Quotable Hollywood.* Barnes and Noble, 2001.

Webster's Dictionary of Quotations. Merriam-Webster, 1992.

Williams, Rose. *Latin Quips at Your Fingertips: Witty Latin Sayings by Wise Romans.* Barnes and Noble, 2000.

Winokur, Jon. *The Portable Curmudgeon.* Jon. New American Library, 1987.

Winkour, Jon. *Zen to Go.* New American Library, 1989.

Winkour, Jon. *The Traveling Curmudgeon.* Sasquatch Books, 2003.

Yong-chol, Kim. *Proverbs East and West: An Anthology of Chinese, Korean, and Japanese Saying with Western Equivalents.* Hollym, 1991.

Zubko, Andy. *Treasury of Spiritual Wisdom: A Collection of 10,000 Inspirational Quotations.* Blue Dove Press.1996.

The internet has dramatically expanded our access to quotations. Six websites deserve to be mentioned as outstanding sources:

- www.bartleby.com/quotations
- www.qotd.org
- www.quotationspage.com
- www.thinkexist.com
- http://en.wikiquote.org
- http://nobelprize.org

About the Authors

ERIC H. ROTH

Eric H. Roth teaches international graduate students the pleasures and perils of academic writing and public speaking in English at the University of Southern California (USC). He also consults English language schools on communicative methods to effectively teach English.

Given a full scholarship as a Lilly Scholar, Roth studied philosophy and American history at Wabash College (1980-1984), and received his M.A. in Media Studies from the New School (1988). Since 1992, Roth has taught English to high school, community college, adult, and university students. Highlights of his career include: teaching the first Saturday morning citizenship class in Santa Monica (1994); directing the CES Adult Education Center (1995-1998); working with international students in summer IEP programs at UCLA Extension (1997-2000, 2003-2005); teaching USC engineering students in Madrid, Spain (2007) and Paris, France (2008); and directing the APU International High School in Ho Chi Minh City, Vietnam (2009).

Roth co-authored *Compelling Conversations: Questions and Quotations on Timeless Topics* in 2006 to help English language learners increase their English fluency. Recommended by *English Teaching Professional* magazine, the advanced ESL textbook has been used in over 40 countries in English classrooms and conversation clubs. *Easy English Times*, an adult literacy newspaper, has published a monthly column, "Instant Conversation Activities," based on the book since 2008. The first specific version for a particular country, Vietnam, was published in 2011. Future versions for Japan, Korea, Israel, Mexico, and Romania are anticipated.

A member of the USC faculty since 2003, Roth is a member of numerous professional organizations including: California Association of Teaching English to Speakers of Other Languages (CATESOL); the International Communication Association (ICA); the International Professors Project (IPP); and Teaching English to Speakers of Other Languages (TESOL). Roth has given several CATESOL conference presentations and led many teacher training workshops.

Roth first visited Vietnam in 2000, and has returned three times to consult and teach. He looks forward to learning more about Vietnam and engaging in many compelling conversations with Vietnamese in the future.

TONI ABERSON

After 35 years of teaching English and supervising English teachers, Toni Aberson (M.A. English; M.A. Psychology and Religion) believes that a lively classroom is the optimal learning environment.

"If people are thinking, sharing, and laughing, then they're learning," notes Aberson. "The mere fact that those adults are in an English classroom attests to their courage and their determination to learn."

"Adult English students bring a wealth of interesting experiences with them," continues Aberson. "They bring the world into the classroom. The challenge for English teachers is to put students at ease and encourage them to practice English. What better way than to ask students about their lives? I love teaching English."

Aberson has launched a new Chimayo Press series for ESL students. *Lively ESL Lessons: American Idioms and More* focuses on real life expressions and situations.

"The key in a classroom is engagement," Aberson says, "and people become interested and excited when they're learning about the daily stuff of life. When they are thinking and writing and talking about their real lives—food, jobs, family, homes, sports, movies—that's when they learn the language. Learning English is not easy. It can be a real challenge, but it can also be fun and stimulating. That's what I'm aiming for—the real life and the fun that stimulates ESL students so they want to learn more. They want to jump in."

P.S. Eric Roth calls Toni "mom."

About this Book and the Series

Compelling Conversations: Questions and Quotations for Advanced Vietnamese English Language Learners is based on our original and highly successful English as a Second Language (ESL) textbook, *Compelling Conversations*. The difference is this unique textbook was created for Vietnamese English Language Learners. Like the original, this English as a Foreign Language (EFL) textbook includes thematic chapters to create quality conversations with conversation starters, interview questions, classic quotations, paraphrasing exercises, and traditional proverbs to create hours of English conversation and class discussions.

This culturally sensitive text encourages students to speak about their experiences, their families, and their lives in Vietnam. With dozens of practical speaking exercises, *Compelling Conversations* helps advanced Vietnamese English Language Learners develop greater fluency, develop and express their opinions, give reasons to support their opinions, build critical thinking skills, prepare for standardized tests with speaking sections (TOEFL, IELTS), and create authentic conversations.

Fluency also requires practice. *Compelling Conversations* encourages students to learn by doing and continually practice speaking English. As a result, students gain greater confidence, fluency, and vocabulary. They also create better conversations in English—in and beyond their English classes.

Originally designed for community college students (ages 18-87!), the textbook has been adopted by American adult schools, international high schools, English language schools and intensive English language programs, university ESL programs, and conversation clubs. Recommended by *English Teaching Professional* magazine, the original, *Compelling Conversations: Questions & Quotations on Timeless Topics* is used by English Language Learners in over 40 countries.

This communicative, oral skills EFL/ESL textbook has been primarily designed for international high schools, community college/university English language programs, and adult education programs. The book combines focused communicative activities and the natural language approach.

We are Chimayo Press, an independent educational publishing company based in Los Angeles since 2005. We're committed to publishing educational and specialty books that create compelling conversations, deepen relationships, and celebrate the human spirit. *Compelling Conversations: Questions & Quotations for Advanced Vietnamese English Language Learners* is the second title in our Compelling Conversations series.

Chimayo Press plans to release additional specialized editions of *Compelling Conversations* for Japan, Korea, Israel, Mexico, and Business Professionals. We will also publish *Lively ESL Lessons: American Idioms and More* in 2011.

We're interested in your feedback and suggestions. Visit us at www.CompellingConversations.com. To discuss special orders, please call +1(310)390–0131 or email eric@compellingconversations.com.

Compelling Conversations: Questions and Quotations for Advanced Vietnamese English Language Learners includes:

- 15 thematic chapters.
- Over 75 communicative activities.
- Partner, group, and class discussion activities to develop fluency.
- 15 targeted vocabulary lists to expand working vocabulary in social, professional, and academic contexts.
- 15 paraphrasing exercises.
- Over 125 global proverbs to build intercultural understanding.
- 15 question writing exercises.
- 150 classic quotations to display eloquent language and develop critical thinking skills.
- 27 black-and-white photographs.
- Versatile material than can be adapted to multi-level listening and speaking classes.
- Critical thinking activities that develop vital academic skills for mainstream college courses.
- Discussion activities to build fluency and classroom speaking skills.
- 18 reproducible out-of-classroom and online assignments for homework.
- An alphabetized academic word list.
- Bibliography.
- 108 pages.

Proof